The Devotions of St. Anselm

The Devotions of St. Anselm

Archbishop of Canterbury

The Devotions of St. Anselm

© Lighthouse Publishing 2019

Written by: St. Anselm (1033 – 1109)
Edited by Clement C.J. Webb (June 25, 1865 – October 5, 1954
Updated into Modern U.S English by A.M. Overett, B.A., REL.
(b. 1960)

Originally published in 1903

All rights reserved. Without limiting the rights under copyright reserved above, no part of this publication may be reproduced, stored in a retrieval system, or transmitted, in any form or by any means (electronic, mechanical, photocopying, recording or otherwise), without the prior written permission of the copyright owner of this book.

Published by
Lighthouse Christian Publishing
SAN 257-4330
5531 Dufferin Drive
Savage, Minnesota, 55378
United States of America

www.lighthousechristianpublishing.com

INTRODUCTION

THE life of Saint Anselm is well known. It belongs to the history of England. By nature a recluse and a thinker, he was called upon to play an active part in political life under circumstances of great difficulty. In the midst of these he bore himself with a conscientious up rightness, a quiet dignity and a persistency in the refusal to sacrifice principle to expediency which justified those who called him against his will to the throne of Canterbury: but his heart was elsewhere, in that passionate search for the innermost meaning of his religious belief, of which the history of the Church affords no more striking example than his. The quarrels about investitures, about the relations of Church and State, of Pope and King, which distracted his outward life in his later years, have left no trace in his writings. In a selection from these, intended to form part of a Library of Devotion, we need not dwell long upon them.

The only one of the works here translated, the date of whose composition is known to us, was written before Anselm was archbishop, while he was still living in the seclusion of his abbey at Bec in Normandy. Even of this earlier part of his life information is so ready to hand that I do not propose to give here more than a very brief account of it. The following outline will be sufficient to inform the reader what manner of man the author was, whose devotions are put before him.

Anselm was born in 1033 at Aosta in

Piedmont, a Burgundian city of Roman origin, governed by its own prince-bishops, and lying at the Italian end of the road over the pass of the Great St Bernard. Both his parents were of noble rank, and his mother, Ermenburga, was a kinswoman of the counts of Maurienne, from whom the house of Savoy, who now sit on the throne of Italy, are descended. A pious and studious boyhood, during which he twice begged for admission to the monastic life from an abbot of his acquaintance, who twice refused him for fear of offending his father, was succeeded by a time in which indulgence in the pleasures of youth diverted him from more serious courses and called down upon him, after the restraining influence of his mother had been withdrawn by her death, the undiscriminating indignation of his father. Finding that nothing he could do availed to win back his father's favor, he at last turned his back upon home and kindred and, with one attendant, set out across the Mont Cenis, to seek a new career beyond the Alps; and so came at last to Bec, drawn by the fame of his countryman, the Lombard scholar Lanfranc of Pavia, then a monk at Bec, afterwards Archbishop of Canterbury and chief counsellor of William the Conqueror. He was himself professed in the same monastery, being now twenty-seven years of age; and soon, in 1063, succeeded Lanfranc, who was then promoted to be Abbot of Duke William's newly founded Abbey of St Stephen at Caen, in the office of Prior; in which capacity he was, owing to the great age of the founder-abbot Herlwin, the principal governor of the society.

In 1078 Herlwin died, and Anselm was elected his successor. The conquest of England by the Norman Duke William in 1066 had brought with it an accession to the abbey of property in that country, which it became the duty of Anselm occasionally to visit. On one of these visits it was that he persuaded his old master Lanfranc, who in 1070 had been raised to the Archbishopric of Canterbury, of the propriety, concerning which Lanfranc had doubted, of recognizing as a martyr his predecessor Alphege, who had been put to death by the heathen Danes, not expressly for refusing to deny the faith of Christ, but because he would not suffer his flock to be impoverished by providing a ransom for him. Anselm, we are told, defended the right of Alphege to the glorious title of martyr as one who had died for righteousness, as the Baptist for truth, and therefore both alike for Christ, who is very truth and very righteousness.

The visits of Anselm to England led to his being held in great reverence there, and at last to his name being pressed upon the Conqueror's son and successor William Rufus, when terrified by a sickness thought to be mortal into a resolution of filling the vacant primacy, which since Lanfranc's death in 1089 he had kept vacant in order to enjoy its revenues. This was in the spring of 1093, and in December of that year Anselm, who much against his will had accepted the king's nomination, was consecrated to the see of St Augustine. From this time onwards his life was one long struggle in defense of ecclesiastical rights and liberties against the masterful sons of the Conqueror. A very few words on the controversy respecting investitures must suffice in this place: but a few are needful, because Anselm's part therein may sometimes alienate from him the sympathy of those in our days who do not comprehend what was thought to be at stake.

As with many of the important struggles of history, an external consideration of this controversy suggests that it was trivial and vexatious; and it is necessary to enter into the point of view of an age very different from our own, to understand its true inner nature. No doubt the conferring of certain ornamental symbols of ecclesiastical dignity is a matter which by itself seems hardly worth the public distress which ensued from the quarrel concerning it; no doubt the predecessor of Anselm had accepted investiture from the predecessor of William Rufus, and the Conqueror had exercised with the consent of Lanfranc, and without the active interference even of so energetic a pope as Gregory VII. himself, the famous Hildebrand, privileges the right to which Anselm would not recognize in the Conqueror's successors; no doubt, as has been pointed out, the Roman See ultimately conceded all over Europe to Christian princes, in substance if not in form, what was refused to them by the popes during the quarrel of the eleventh and twelfth centuries. Did then Anselm waste his life on an unimportant contest? I think not. If some of the most enlightened minds of those times took uncompromisingly the

Roman side in the quarrel, undeterred very often by a clear perception that the actual policy of the Roman See was often inconsistent and even venal, it was that they saw in the independence of the ecclesiastical order under its Roman chief the security and the one security for the maintenance of the Christian moral code in a half-barbarous age of violence and sensuality. The feudal customs of the European nations, however deeply modified by Christian influence, rested on no intelligible Christian or even rational principle; and so not only the canon law but the Roman civil law also, with its claims to rationality and universality, might well seem sacred and divine in contrast to the chaotic "common law" of the nations. Thus in the next century after Anselm's the great scholar John of Salisbury could compare the sin of King Stephen in suppressing Vacarius' lectures on the Roman law in England and in confiscating Archbishop Theobald's copy of Justinian with the impieties of Uzziah and Antiochus Epiphanes. There was no guarantee that a king would uphold the moral law of Christendom; or William the Conqueror, who for all his masterfulness cared above all things for the authority and effectiveness of the church in his dominions, might be succeeded by a reckless and godless son like William Rufus: whereas, though the series of popes would no less display inequalities of moral excellence, the whole raison d'être, as we say, of a pope's position, whatever his personal character, was that of the upholder of the Christian law; it rested ultimately not, like a king's, on force, but on general veneration for

Christianity, however imperfectly understood. The example of the subjection of the Church at Constantinople to the civil power was a warning not to be forgotten against a like submissiveness in the west. We must not forget moreover that the people often recognized the cause of the clergy and the Church as their own, as that of the oppressed against the oppressor; this was probably the secret of Becket's popularity, which had nothing to do, as the French historian Augustin Thierry supposed, with a Saxon origin which was not his; and the like popularity attended Anselm, who was not even born in the country; thus on occasion of a demonstration of popular sympathy with him Eadmer his biographer observes, "We rejoiced therefore and took heart, trusting that, as the Scripture saith, The voice of the people is the voice of God."

Thus much I have said about the controversy concerning investitures, because the quarrel about the rights of King and Pope occupied so important a place in Anselm's life that some understanding of that quarrel is indispensable to a sympathetic appreciation of the man.

In 1097 Anselm, against the will of the king, but, as he conceived, in accordance with his duty, left England to visit the Pope, Urban II., who received him with great honor, and carried him with him the following year to the council of Bari, where Anselm disputed against the representatives of the Greek Church on the doctrine of the procession of the Holy Ghost, as to which, in consequence of his work, addressed to Pope Urban, On the Trinity and the Incarnation of the Word he was already reckoned a high authority, and on which he afterwards composed an important treatise, which we still possess. In 1099 he was present at another council at Rome, where severe censures were pronounced against those who, being laymen, gave or who received from laymen investiture with ecclesiastical office. Anselm, with his already high notions of papal authority, was by his assent to the decrees of this council plunged deeper than before into the controversy of which I spoke above. He had quarreled with William Rufus, mainly because he held that it was his right and duty to recognize the authority of him whom he judged the lawful pope in England, apart from any royal recognition, while the king, taking advantage of the circumstance that there were two claimants of the Roman See, maintained that the recognition in his dominions of any particular person as pope belonged to the royal prerogative. He had not hitherto objected to all investiture with ecclesiastical office by lay men, and had himself done homage to William Rufus for the archbishopric of Canterbury as Lanfranc had done to the Conqueror. But now, when recalled by Henry I. on William's death in the year after the council of Rome—1100,—he refused this homage, and in 1103 left England again to take counsel of Urban's successor, Paschal II. He was reconciled with Henry,—who was not, like his brother, a hater and willful oppressor of the Church,—in 1106, partly through the mediation of Adela, Countess of Blois, the king's sister and mother of his successor Stephen, one of many devout women of rank, among whom Henry's own queen, Maud, must be reckoned, who were profoundly attached to Anselm as a spiritual guide. He returned to England in 1107, died on April 21, 1109, at Canterbury, and was buried in his cathedral church next to the tomb of his master, friend, and predecessor, Lanfranc.

Such is the bare outline of this great man's life. Of the beauties of his character, his self-devotion, his gentleness, his equanimity, his kindliness and tolerance, I have said nothing; they will be found set forth in the contemporary Latin life by Eadmer, with the charm that only an admiring friend can give to the story of one he has known and almost worshipped. For modern biographies of Anselm I would refer to the French scholar Charles de Rémusat's lucid and thoughtful monograph Anselme de Canterbury, to the full and learned, if somewhat diffuse and fanciful work of Mr. Martin Rule, Life and Times of St Anselm, to Dean Church's well-known sketch, to the careful article by Dean Stephens in the Dictionary of National Biography, and the charmingly-written chapter by Mr. J. R. Green in his Short History of the English People.

The first treatise of Anselm's which I have chosen to translate is the greatest of all his works, the Proslogion, as he called it, or Address to God, in which he sought to show how by one irrefragable argument the being of God could be demonstrated against all who should say with the fool in the Psalms, There is no God. It was not without much hesitation that I included the Proslogion in this selection. For it deals with an abstruse subject-matter, and though it deals with it in a style singularly simple, and almost wholly free from technical expressions, it is beyond doubt difficult to understand without a considerable effort of attention and thought. But it seemed to me that no selection from Anselm's devotional works could be considered representative, which did not include this very remarkable writing. For the justification of including Anselm among the masters of devotional literature lies in this, that no one has ever more strikingly shown how the disinterested search for metaphysical truth can be offered as a service of passionate devotion to God. The saying of Hegel, Das Denken ist auch Gottesdienst, might be the motto of the most part of Anselm's writings. The more richly endowed and many-sided intelligence of Augustine, in virtue of the very variety and breadth of its interests, illustrates less remarkably than that of Anselm "the saint as philosopher." The story of Anselm's death bed tells its own tale of the dominance of speculative interest in his spiritual life. "Palm Sunday had dawned," so Eadmer reports it, "and we were sitting round him according to our custom; one of us therefore said to him, 'Lord and Father, we understand that you are leaving the world and going to your Lord's Easter court.' He answered, 'If indeed this is His will, I will gladly obey His will. But if He should rather please that I should still remain among you at least long enough to be able to finish the working-out of a problem, which I am revolving in my mind, concerning the origin of the soul, I could gratefully accept it, in that I know not whether any will finish it, when I am gone.'" The Proslogion, the principal monument of such a character, may thus be regarded as a work of high devotional as well as of high philosophical value. As a work of devotion it seemed to me not to need an elaborate philosophical commentary; I have, however, added in a supplementary Note some few observations upon the reasoning which it contains. The reader who cares enough for metaphysical speculation to follow them with attention will not fail to go further. It is probably true that the "ontological argument," as the argument of the Proslogion afterwards came to be called, is open to objection in the form which Anselm gave to it; and that, even if it does prove something, it does not prove all which Anselm intended it to prove. The contemporary criticism of the monk Gaunilo in his Apology for the Fool Anselm himself answered in a treatise which is a model at once of metaphysical acuteness and of controversial courtesy; Kant's criticism of the same argument, as it was revived at the inauguration of modern philosophy by Descartes, is a graver matter, and, however we may think that Kant may be answered on this point or on that, no doubt he showed the bankruptcy of all merely logical arguments to prove the existence of the God of religion. But the devotional value of the Proslogiondoes not stand or fall with the adequacy or inadequacy of the argument it contains; a perception of the inadequacy of the argument may even lend it a greater devotional value. Devout persons will often welcome a supposed proof of the truth of what they believe, less because they need proof for themselves, than because they wish to be able to silence objectors; and, if only the objectors are silenced, they are often not very careful to examine too closely the means by which it is done. Thus they fall into the error of the scholasticism which roused the indignation of Bacon, the scholasticism which seeks not the truth but only the refutation of an opponent. They became impatient with the philosophical enquirer who has an eye for difficulties, and is never done grubbing up the roots of his convictions. And the philosophical enquirer is apt on his side to fall out of sympathy with the devout, and all the more so if they adorn their doctrine with the language of a philosophy which is to them no more than apologetics. In Anselm's Proslogion, however, he will not find apologetics but genuine enquiry; yet this enquiry is conducted in a spirit of the most profound devotion. This may seem a strange claim to make for a treatise whose alternative title is Faith in search of Understanding, and which contains the famous saying, Credo ut intelligam, I believe in order that I may understand. Is not this the very opposite of free enquiry, to make faith the starting-point? I do not think so. A philosophy of religion is as little attainable without a religious experience, which the philosopher first has, and then endeavors to understand, as a philosophy of aesthetic without an experience denied to one who is insusceptible to the beauty of nature and of art. It is this living religious experience, rather than merely the acquiescence in an authoritative dogma, that Anselm has in view when he speaks of faith. No doubt to him, living in an age when only one creed was practically presented to his mind, the distinction between these two meanings of faith was not obvious as it is to us. But I do not believe that an acquaintance with the writings of Anselm at first hand will allow a candid reader to see in him a mere apologist. He has much of the same originality and independence of mind, the same aptitude for introspection, as the reviver of his argument, Descartes; and as a philosopher of religion he has the advantage of the modern thinker in a far richer and more thorough religious experience with which to start.

The story of the composition of the Proslogionis thus told by Anselm's companion and biographer, the monk Eadmer. "After this it came into his mind to enquire whether it would be possible to demonstrate by one short argument alone what is believed and taught concerning God, namely, that He is eternal, unchangeable, almighty, everywhere wholly present, in comprehensible, righteous, gracious, merciful, true, truth, goodness, righteousness, and so forth, and how all these attributes are one in Him. And this matter, as he told us, he found one of great difficulty. For the consideration thereof not only often robbed him of appetite and of sleep but, which vexed him more, distracted the direction of his thoughts to God at matins and at other services of the Church. When therefore he perceived this, and could not fully achieve the discovery of that which he sought, he concluded that this train of thought was a temptation of the devil, and strove to dismiss it from his mind. But the more he labored to do this, the more did the thought haunt his mind. And all at once one night during the office of nocturns[8] the grace of God shone into his heart, and the thing which he sought became plain to his understanding, and filled all his inward parts with an infinite joy and delight. Considering then in himself that the same reasoning if it were known to others might be pleasing to them also, he did not grudge them this satisfaction, but wrote down his argument on tablets and delivered them to a brother of the monastery for more careful custody. When some days had passed, he asked this brother for the tablets. Search was made in the place where they had been put by, but they could not be found. The brethren were asked after them, lest one of them should have taken them, but in vain. Nor could anyone be found who acknowledged that he had known anything of them. Then Anselm wrote another discourse concerning the same matter on other tablets, and delivered them to the same brother to be kept more carefully. The brother laid them up in the innermost part of his bedchamber, and the next day, though he had no suspicion of any mischief, found them lying about on the floor in front of his bed, the wax broken into fragments and scattered on every side. The tablets were picked up, the wax collected, and brought to Anselm; he put together the wax and, though with difficulty, recovered the writing. But fearing lest it should altogether be lost through carelessness, he commanded that it should be transcribed on parchment in the name of the Lord. And so he composed a book, small in bulk but great in the importance of the wise judgments and subtle reasonings which it contained, and this he called Proslogion or The Address. For herein he addresses either himself or God throughout. Now this work came into the hands of a certain person, who was not a little dissatisfied with some of the reasoning therein, and thinking it insufficient, desired to refute it. He composed therefore a treatise against it and wrote it at the end of Anselm's own work. This was then sent to Anselm by a friend; and when he had considered it, he was glad, and thanking his censor, he devised an answer to the censure, and adding that to the treatise which had been sent him, he returned to the friend who had sent it the censure and the reply together, in the hope that not only this friend but others who desired to possess his book, would wish it so, that to his own work should be added the censure of his reasoning, and to the censure his own answer thereunto."

The critic whose adverse judgment of his treatise Anselm received with such pleasure (showing thereby how far more he was in love with the truth than with his own opinion) is known to have been Gaunilo, a monk of Marmoutier, whose work under the title An Apology for the Fool (that is, for the Psalmist's fool who said, There is no God) is still found in editions of Anselm following the Proslogion, and followed in its turn by Anselm's rejoinder.

To the Proslogion I have added renderings of certain of the Meditations, Prayers, and Letters of Anselm. My choice has been made with a view to the devotion of Anglican Christians of to-day, for whom this series is primarily intended. I have thus not chosen for translation meditations and prayers, the language of which would be entirely uncongenial to modern Anglican feeling, prayers (for example) addressed to St Mary or to other saints. But what I have chosen, I have given in full.

I take this opportunity of acknowledging with grateful thanks the help which I have received in the preparation of this book for the press from my sister, Miss Mildred Webb, and from my friend, Mr. Guy Kendall, of Magdalen College, who read the whole of it in proof.

St Anselm does not appear to me to rank, except in one kind, that of which the Proslogion is an example, among the great masters of devotional literature. His meditations and prayers are often indeed characteristic of their writer. The student of his theological and philosophical works will often notice in them phrases which show how deeply his thought entered into his personal religion and colored its expression. They are in spirit exceedingly free from any taint of superstition; in many of his prayers addressed to saints there is a perfunctoriness and conventionality which show that, while he could use on occasion without misgiving the language of a view which made of

God the image of an earthly king whose ear might be gained by the means of powerful favorites at court, this kind of devotion remained somewhat external to his inner life, the truer expression of which is found elsewhere in prayers which breathe a genuinely evangelical spirit of trust in God through Christ alone.

The second Meditation (which I have included in this selection) is especially admired by Mr. Rule. It is a striking example of medieval piety in one of its most characteristic moods. In it a profound horror of sin and an intimate sense of personal sinfulness find expression under the vividly realized scriptural imagery of a great assize. Those who are acquainted with the history of Luther will remember how the great thought of justification by faith alone came to him as a deliverance from the spirit of distrustful and unloving anxiety which was a natural temptation of the monastic life. Isolated from the ordinary occupations, duties, and trials of human life, spending much time in self-examination, inspired with the ambition to exemplify as perfectly as possible in his own person a certain somewhat one-sided ideal of living, which was deliberately regarded as an ideal in itself higher than that of the secular Christian, the earnest religious had much to invite him now to a reliance on his own works, now (by reaction) to an unrelieved horror of the judgment which must be passed by a perfectly just Judge on an obedience so imperfect as self-examination showed him that his was. Thus the terror of the Lord has perhaps more than its due place in works of the class to which St Anselm's second Meditation belongs. Nevertheless this fear and horror of judgment is a normal stage in the development of the Christian life. Even where the Christian life has advanced beyond it, the moods of the Christian, like those of other men, are not always on a level with his highest spiritual attainment. The sincere expression of an important part of spiritual experience does not quickly lose its value, even though its form have fallen out of fashion. It has often been remarked that the middle ages, in their preoccupation with the thought of Christ as Judge, sometimes forgot to think of Him as Savior, and therefore devised other mediators to stand between the guilty sinner and His wrath; and many representations of the Last Judgment in art give support to this observation. But however this may be, in this work of St Anselm's there is no such matter; he flies for refuge only to the Judge who is at the same time his Savior.

The same is even more emphatically true of our third (Gerberon's sixth) Meditation. This is written in a style more simple than Anselm's is wont to be, but it is well attested for his, and is conceived entirely in his spirit. Through whatever changes the language of Christian devotion has passed or is yet to pass, the revelation of God in the life and death of Jesus Christ has been and is to thousands of Christians as to Anselm here, a revelation at once of sin condemned and salvation freely offered, in the light of which no thought either of the bargaining which derogates from the holiness of God, or of the merit which gives an occasion to human pride, can for a moment find a place.

Our fourth Meditation (Gerberon's eleventh) is thoroughly characteristic of Anselm. In great part it embodies the doctrine of the Atonement which is set forth at length in his famous theological work Cur Deus Homo. That doctrine is open to the charge of conceiving the whole matter from a legal standpoint, which gives to the notions connected with the owing and paying of debts an ultimate and absolute value that they cannot possess. It holds, however, an important place in the history of theology by reason of its decided rejection of the views which some had put forward that the death of Christ was a price paid to the devil, or even a trick played upon him. The latter view Anselm sees clearly to be inconsistent with holding God to be the Truth; it is indeed a low and heathenish notion, already before the days of Christianity condemned by Plato, who made it a canon of theology to attribute no deceitfulness to God. But even the theory that a price due to the devil had to be paid was false; for it gave to the power of evil an independent place over against God which believers in One God could not consistently concede to it. These theories Anselm rightly puts aside; but his own theory also falls short of what is required in a doctrine of the Atonement. It does not turn upon the love of God, but, as was said above, upon a legal conception of His justice. Distinctions between the divine and the human nature, between the Redeemer and the redeemed, are more present to his thought (though not to his feeling) than the unity in which the religious experience of reconciliation and atonement finds them overcome. Yet it must not be forgotten that the Christian sense of forgiveness differs from that which might be enjoyed by one who thought of God as a kindly being who forgets, rather than forgives, what is done amiss, just in this very point, that for the Christian full justice (as we say) is done to the forgiven sin; it is faced, known, "naked and open to the eyes of Him with whom we have to do." Thus forgiven, it is indeed, as sin, taken away; whereas, were it only passed over and ignored, it might be there still, poisoning the air; we should not really have done with it. A deep sense of sin and a genuine faith in its remission go together. Hence the readiness of the true penitent to bear the punishment of his sin, so he may be rid of the sin; the false penitent desires less to be rid of the sin than to escape the punishment. It is this aspect of the experience of atonement to which Anselm's language about a debt to be paid aims at giving expression.

 Into the history of these devotional writings of Anselm I have not thought it my business to enter here. It will be found perhaps most fully treated by Mr. Rule; or in the "Historical Notice " prefixed by Dr Pusey to a translation of Meditations and Prayers addressed to the Holy Trinity and our Lord Jesus Christ by S. Anselm, sometime Archbishop of Canterbury, which was published by Parker at Oxford in 1856. I have translated from Gerberon's edition, which is reprinted in Migne's Patrologia Latina. The translation is a new one; but it is not in all cases the first offered to English readers. In 1708 Dean Stanhope of Canterbury published a book called Pious Breathings, Being the Meditations of St Augustine, his Treatise of the Love of God, Soliloquies and Manual, to which are added Select Contemplations from St Anselm and St Bernard: and in 1856 appeared the Oxford translation mentioned above, under the auspices of Dr Pusey. To this last I have occasionally been indebted for a word or phrase.

The devotion of St Anselm is of course the devotion of his age and circumstances. He was a monk, and his Christianity has a monastic cast; those who use this series for the most part take their share in the occupations of family, social, civil life, and their Christianity is affected by their experience as Anselm's was by his. The tone neither of his Christianity nor of theirs is exactly that of the New Testament. In one point the Christianity of the Middle Ages and that of our own time are alike contrasted with that of the Apostles; both recognize, ours, however, more completely than that of the middle ages, that the scientific life and the political life are spheres in which Christians may be expected to move. In another point our Christianity is contrasted with the medieval and the apostolic, in that there, and especially in medieval Christianity, the imagination dealt more confidently with the hopes and fears of a future life than is easy or possible for us. But, in spite of all this, there is a fundamental likeness among all the products of the Christian spirit: in all there is a contempt of the world which is not proud or bitter, but humbled by the consciousness of sin, and sweetened by the love of Christ. We have much reason to fear the warning addressed to those who say Lord, Lord, and do not the things that He said; but even to say Lord, Lord, to Christ, is to own a standard and an ideal which are not those of this world. The discontent with what falls short of that standard and that ideal, which it is the function of devotional writing to arouse, is aroused by Anselm in tones which are, as I have already suggested, especially worthy the attention of those whose natural bent is towards philosophical reflection. Two opposite dangers beset such persons: the indulgence in contemplation, which weakens the sense of personal sinfulness; and the fear of consequences, which refuses to follow the argument, in Plato's words, whithersoever it leads us. The study of Anselm, a pattern of humble penitence and of indefatigable intellectual curiosity, should discourage both these perilous tendencies, and encourage at once sound thought and genuine devotion.

PROSLOGION
OR ADDRESS TO GOD CONCERNING HIS EXISTENCE

PREFACE

I FORMERLY published, at the instance of certain of my brethren, a little work, in which, assuming the person of one who by silent reasoning with himself is searching for a knowledge he does not yet possess, I gave an example of the manner in which we may meditate concerning the grounds of our faith. But afterwards, when I considered that this work was put together by the interweaving of a great number of arguments, I began to ask myself whether there might not perhaps be found someone argument which should have no need of any other argument beside itself to prove it, and might suffice by itself to demonstrate that God really exists and is the Supreme Good, which needed nothing beside itself to give it being or well-being, but without which nothing else can have either the one or the other; and whereof all other things are true which we believe concerning the divine essence. And when after many times earnestly directing my thoughts to this matter, it sometimes seemed to me that what I sought was just within my grasp, but sometimes that it eluded my mind's sight altogether, at last I resolved in despair to renounce the search for a thing, the discovery whereof was beyond my powers. But this train of thought, so soon as I desired to lay it aside lest it should hinder my mind while vainly occupied therein from attending to other matters which might be more profitable to me, at once began to press itself as it were importunately upon me, unwilling and reluctant as I was to entertain it. And so one day, when I was wearied out with violently resisting this importunity, in the midst of the struggle of my thoughts, there so presented itself to me the very thing which I had given up hope of finding, that I hastened to embrace that very train of thought which I was but a moment ago anxiously thrusting from me. Thinking therefore that if I wrote down what I so greatly rejoiced to have found, it would please others who might read it, I wrote the following little work, treating of this and of some other matters, in the character of one striving to raise his thoughts to the contemplation of God and seeking to understand what he already believes. And because neither this nor the other treatise which I mentioned before, seemed to me worthy to be called a book or to have the writer's name set in the front of it, and yet I thought I must not let them go without some title to invite those to read into whose hands they might come, I gave a name to each, calling the former An example of meditation on the grounds of faith and the latter Faith in search of Understanding. But, when both had been often transcribed under these titles by divers persons, was constrained by many and especially by Hugh the reverend Archbishop of Lyons and Legate of the Apostolic See in Gaul, who laid his commands upon me in virtue of his apostolical authority, to prefix my name to them. And so that this might be done more fittingly, I have called the former Monologion, that is, The Soliloquy, and this Proslogion, that is, The Address.

CHAPTER I

COME now, thou poor child of man, turn awhile from thy business, hide thyself for a little time from restless thoughts, cast away thy troublesome cares, put aside thy wearisome distractions. Give thyself a little leisure to converse with God, and take thy rest awhile in Him. Enter into the secret chamber of thy heart: leave everything without but God and what may help thee to seek after Him, and when thou hast shut the door, then do thou seek Him. Say now, O my whole heart, say now to God, I seek Thy face; Thy face, Lord, do I seek. Come now then, O Lord my God, teach Thou my heart when and how I may seek Thee, where and how I may find Thee? O Lord, if Thou art not here, where else shall I seek Thee? but if Thou art everywhere, why do I not behold Thee, since Thou art here present? Surely indeed Thou dwells in the light which no man can approach unto. But where is that light unapproachable? or how may I approach unto it since it is unapproachable? or who shall lead me and bring me into it that I may see Thee therein? Again, by what tokens shall I know Thee, in what form shall I look for Thee? I have never seen Thee, O Lord my God; I know not Thy form. What shall I do then, O Lord most high, what shall I do, banished as I am so far from Thee? What shall Thy servant do that is sick for love of Thee, and yet is cast away from Thy presence? He panted to behold Thee, and yet Thy presence is very far from him. He longed to approach unto Thee, and yet Thy dwelling-place is unapproachable. He desired to find Thee, yet he knoweth not Thy habitation. He would fain seek Thee, yet he knoweth not Thy face. O Lord, Thou art my God, Thou art my Lord; and I have never beheld

Thee. Thou hast created me and created me anew, and all good things that I have, hast Thou bestowed upon me, and yet I have never known Thee. Nay, I was created to behold Thee, and yet have I never unto this day done that for the sake whereof I was created. O miserable lot of man, to have lost that whereunto he was created! O hard and terrible condition! Alas, what hath he lost? what hath he found? what hath departed from him? what hath continued with him? He hath lost the blessedness whereunto he was created, and he hath found the misery whereunto he was not created; that without which nothing is happy, hath departed from him, and that hath continued with him which by itself cannot but be miserable. Once man did eat angels' food, after which he now hungered; now he eateth the bread of affliction, which then he knew not. Alas for the common woe of man, the universal sorrow of the children of Adam! Our first father was filled with abundance, we sigh with hunger; he was rich, we are beggars. He miserably threw away that in the possession whereof he was happy, and in the lack whereof we are miserable; after which we lamentably long and alas! Abide unsatisfied. Why did he not keep for us, when he might easily have kept it that the loss whereof so grievously afflicts us? Wherefore did he so overcloud our day, and plunge us into darkness? Why did he take from us our life, and bring upon us the pains of death? Wretches that we are, whence have we been driven out and whither? From our native country into banishment, from the vision of God into blindness, from the joy of immortality into the bitterness and horror of death. How sad the change from so great good to so great evil! Grievous is the loss, grievous the pain, grievous everything. But alas for me, one of the miserable children of Eve, cast far away from God! What did I begin? and what have I accomplished? At what did I aim? and unto what have I attained? To what did I aspire? and where am I now sighing? I sought good, and behold, trouble. I aimed at God, and have stumbled upon myself. I sought rest in my secret chamber, and I have found tribulation and grief in the inmost parts. I desired to laugh for gladness of spirit and am constrained to roar for the disquietness of my heart.6I hoped for joy and behold increase of sorrow. How long, O Lord, how long? How long, O Lord, wilt Thou forget us, how long wilt Thou hide Thy face from us? When wilt Thou turn and hearken unto us? When wilt thou enlighten our eyes and show us Thy face? When wilt Thou restore Thy presence to us? Turn and took upon us, O Lord: hearken unto us, enlighten us, show us Thyself. Restore to us Thy presence that it may be well with us; for without Thee it goeth very ill with us. Have pity upon our labors and strivings after Thee, for without Thee we can do nothing. Thou calls us; help us to obey the call. I beseech Thee, O Lord, that I may not despair in my sighing, but may draw full breath again in hope. My heart is embittered by its desolation; with Thy consolation, I beseech Thee, O Lord, make it sweet again. I beseech Thee, O Lord, for in my hunger I have begun to seek Thee, suffer me not to depart from Thee fasting. I have come to Thee fainting for lack of food; let me not go empty away. I have come to Thee, as the poor man to the rich, as the miserable to the merciful, let me not return unsatisfied and despised: and if before I be fed, I sigh, grant me that, though after I have sighed, I may be fed. O Lord, I am bent downwards, I cannot look up: raise me up, that I may lift mine eyes to heaven. My iniquities are gone over my head, they overwhelm me;

they are like a sore burden too heavy for me to bear.8 Deliver me, take away my burden, lest the pit of my wickedness shut its mouth upon me: grant unto me that I may look upon Thy light, though from afar off, though out of the deep. I will seek Thee, with longing after Thee. I will long after Thee in seeking Thee, I will find Thee by loving Thee, I will love Thee in finding Thee. I confess to Thee, O Lord, and I give thanks unto Thee, because Thou hast created in me this Thine image, that I may remember Thee, think upon Thee, love Thee: but so darkened is Thine image in me by the smoke of my sins that it cannot do that whereunto it was created, unless Thou renew it and create it again. I seek not, O Lord, to search out Thy depth, but I desire in some measure to understand Thy truth, which my heart believeth and loves. Nor do I seek to understand that I may believe, but I believe that I may understand. For this too I believe, that unless I first believe, I shall not understand.

CHAPTER II

THEREFORE, O Lord, who grants to faith understanding, grant unto me that, so far as Thou knows it to be expedient for me, I may understand that Thou art, as we believe; and also that Thou art what we believe Thee to be. And of a truth we believe that Thou art somewhat than which no greater can be conceived. Is there then nothing real that can be thus described? for the fool hath said in his heart, There is no God. Yet surely even that fool himself when he hears me speak of somewhat than which nothing greater can be conceived understands what he hears, and what he understands is in his understanding, even if he do not understand that it really exists. It is one thing for a thing to be in the understanding, and another to understand that the thing really exists. For when a painter considers the work which he is to make, he has it indeed in his understanding; but he doth not yet understand that really to exist which as yet he has not made. But when he has painted his picture, then he both has the picture in his understanding, and also understands it really to exist. Thus even the fool is certain that something exists, at least in his understanding, than which nothing greater can be conceived; because, when he hears this mentioned, he understands it, and whatsoever is understood, exists in the understanding. And surely that than which no greater can be conceived cannot exist only in the understanding. For if it exist indeed in the understanding only, it can be thought to exist also in reality; and real existence is more than existence in the understanding only. If then that than which no greater can be conceived exists in the understanding only, then that than which no greater can be conceived is something a greater than which can be conceived: but this is impossible. Therefore it is certain that something than which no greater can be conceived exists both in the understanding and also in reality.

CHAPTER III

NOT only does this something than which no greater can be conceived exist, but it exists in so true a sense that it cannot even be conceived not to exist. For it is possible to form the conception of an object whose non-existence shall be inconceivable; and such an object is of necessity greater than any object whose existence is conceivable: wherefore if that than which no greater can be conceived can be conceived not to exist; it follows that

that than which no greater can be conceived is not that than which no greater can be conceived [for there can be thought a greater than it, namely, an object whose non-existence shall be inconceivable]; and this brings us to a contradiction. And thus it is proved that that thing than which no greater can be conceived exists in so true a sense, that it cannot even be conceived not to exist: and this thing art Thou, O Lord our God! And so Thou, O Lord my God, exists in so true a sense that Thou canst not even be conceived not to exist. And this is as is fitting. For if any mind could conceive aught better than Thee, then the creature would be ascending above the Creator, and judging the Creator; which is a supposition very absurd. Thou therefore dost exist in a truer sense than all else besides Thee, and art more real than all else besides Thee; because whatsoever else existed, existed in a less true sense than Thou, and therefore is less real than Thou. Why then said the fool in his heart, There is no God, when it is so plain to a rational mind that Thou art more real than anything else? Why, except that he is a fool indeed?

CHAPTER IV

BUT how came the fool to say in his heart that which he could not conceive? or how came he to be able not to conceive that which yet he said in his heart? For it may be thought that to conceive and to say in one's heart are one and the same thing. If it is true—nay, because it is true, that he conceived it, because he said it in his heart; and also true that he did not say it in his heart because he could not conceive it; it follows that there are two senses in which something may be understood to be conceived or said in the heart. For in one sense we are said to have a conception of something, when we have a conception of the word that signifies it; and in another sense, when we understand what the thing really is. In the former sense then we may say that God is conceived not to exist: but in the latter, He cannot by any means be conceived not to exist. For no man that understandeth what fire and water mean, can conceive that fire is really water; though he may have this conception, as far as the words go. Thus in like manner no man that understandeth what God is can conceive that God does not exist; although he may say these words [that God does not exist] either with no meaning at all, or with some other meaning than that which they properly bear. For God is that than which no greater can be conceived. He who well understandeth what this is, certainly understandeth it to be such as cannot even be conceived not to exist. Whosoever therefore understandeth in this way that God exists, cannot conceive that he does not exist. Thanks be to Thee, O good Lord, thanks be to Thee! because that which heretofore I believed by Thy grace, I now by Thine illumination thus understand, so that, even though I should not wish to believe in Thine existence, I cannot but understand that Thou dost exist.

CHAPTER V

WHAT then art Thou Lord God, Thou than which nothing greater can be conceived? What indeed but that Supreme Good which being alone of all things self-existent, didst make all other things beside Thee out of nothing? For whatsoever is not this is less than can be conceived: but Thou canst not be conceived to be less than the highest conceivable. What good thing is lacking to the Supreme Good, whereon depends the being of every good thing beside? Thou therefore art righteous, true, blessed, and hast all attributes which it is better to have than to be without; for it is better to be righteous than not righteous, and blessed than not blessed.

CHAPTER VI

BUT since it is better to have perception or to have omnipotence, to be pitiful or to be without passions, than not to have these attributes; how hast Thou perception, if Thou art not a body? or omnipotence, if Thou canst not do everything? or how art Thou at one and the same time pitiful and without passions? For if only bodily things have perception, since the senses with which we perceive belong and attach to the body; how canst Thou have perception, since Thou art not a body but the Supreme Spirit, which is higher than a body can be? But if perception is only knowledge or a means towards knowledge; since he who perceives, has knowledge thereby, according to the special character of the senses, by sight of colors, by taste of savors and so forth: then whatsoever has knowledge in whatsoever manner may be said without impropriety in some sense to perceive. Therefore, O Lord, although Thou art not a body, yet of a truth Thou hast in this sense perception in the highest degree, since Thou knows all things in the highest degree; but not in the sense wherein an animal that has knowledge by means of bodily feeling is said to have perception.

CHAPTER VII

BUT again, how canst Thou be omnipotent, if

Thou canst not do all things? Yet if Thou canst not suffer corruption, canst not lie, canst not make what is true to be false, or what is done, undone, and so forth; how canst Thou do all things? Or shall we say that to be capable of these would be not power but rather impotence? For he who can do these, can do what is not expedient for him, and what he ought not; and the more he can do what is not expedient for him and what he ought not, the more power have evil and wickedness over him, and the less power hath he against them. He therefore that can do such things, can do them in virtue not of power but of impotence. For he is said to be able to do them, not because he himself has power in doing them, but because his impotence gives something else power to work in him; or else in an improper way of speaking, such as we often use when we put to be for not to be, and to do for not to door to do nothing. For we often say to one who says that a thing is not such-and-such: It is as you say it is; when it would seem more proper to say, It is not as you say it is not. Again we say: This man sits, as that man does; or This man rests as that man does: though sitting is a kind of not doing, and resting is doing nothing. Thus then when a man is said to have the power of doing or undergoing what is not expedient for him or what he ought not, the word power signifies impotence; since the more power of this sort he hath, the more power have evil and wickedness against him, and the less hath he against them. Therefore, O Lord God, Thou art all the more truly omnipotent, that Thou canst do nothing that is done through impotence, and nothing hath any power against Thee.

CHAPTER VIII

ONCE again, how art Thou at the same time pitiful and yet without passions? For unless Thou have passions, Thou wilt not have compassion; if Thou hast not compassion, Thy heart is not made sorry by compassion, that is by fellow-feeling with the sorrowful; and this is what pity is. Yet if Thou art not pitiful, whence have the sorrowful so great consolation from Thee? How then canst Thou at once be and not be pitiful, O Lord, unless because Thou art pitiful in respect of us, and art not pitiful in respect of Thyself? For Thou art pitiful to our apprehension, and art not pitiful to Thine own. For when Thou hast respect to us in our sorrow, we perceive the effects of pity; but Thou feels not the emotion thereof. And thus Thou art pitiful in that Thou savest the wretched, and sparest those that sin against Thee; and yet again Thou art not moved by a fellow-feeling with our misery.

CHAPTER IX

AGAIN, how dost Thou spare the wicked, if Thou art wholly and supremely just? For how dost Thou, being wholly and supremely just, do aught that is not just? And what manner of justice is that, to give eternal life to one that deserves eternal death? Whence then, O good God, good both to the good and to the evil, whence is it that Thou savest the evil, if to save the evil is not just, and yet Thou does nothing that is not just? Or is it because Thy goodness is incomprehensible that this lieth hid in that light unapproachable which is Thy dwelling place? Verily it is in the most deep and secret abyss of Thy goodness that there lieth hid the fountain, whence flowed the river

St. Anselm

of Thy mercy. For though Thou art wholly and supremely just, yet art Thou also gracious to the wicked, because Thou art wholly and supremely good. For Thou wouldest be less good, if Thou wert not gracious to any that was evil. For better is he who is good both to the good and to the evil than he who is good to the good only; and better is he who is good to the evil both in punishing and in sparing them, than he who is good in punishing them only. Therefore Thou art pitiful because Thou art wholly and supremely good. And although perchance we suppose that we see reason why Thou dost reward good to the good and evil to the evil, yet certainly we must be filled with wonder why Thou, being wholly and supremely just and having need of nothing, renders good to the evil and those who have sinned against Thee. O the depth of Thy goodness, O God! We both see whence Thou art merciful and yet see it only in part. We perceive whence the river flows, yet behold not the fountain from which it springs. For it is of the plenitude of Thy goodness, that Thou art kind to them that have sinned against Thee; and yet it lieth hid in the depth of Thy goodness wherefore this is so. Verily although it is in Thy goodness that Thou rewards good to the good, and evil to the evil; yet this the rule of justice seems to require. But when Thou rewards good to the evil, then we know that the supremely Good willed to do that, yet wonder that the supremely Just was able so to will. O thou mercy of God, from how abundant a sweetness, from how sweet an abundance flows thou forth unto us! O boundless goodness of God, how ought we sinners to be moved by love of Thee! For Thou savest the just, justice assenting; but delivers the wicked, when justice condemns them; Thou savest the just by the help of their deserts; Thou delivers the wicked against their deserts; Thou savest the just, acknowledging in them the good which Thou didst give them; Thou delivers the wicked, pardoning the evil which Thou hates. O immeasurable goodness, passing all understanding, let that mercy be shed upon me, which proceeded from the great riches of that goodness! Let there flow into me that mercy which flowed out of that goodness. Spare in Thy mercy, and take not vengeance in Thy justice. For although it be hard to understand how Thy mercy is not parted from Thy justice; yet is it necessary to believe that it is not at enmity with Thy justice, that it flowed from Thy goodness, that it is not without justice, nay in truth accorded with Thy justice. For if Thou art merciful only because Thou art supremely good, and art supremely good only because Thou art supremely just: therefore art Thou in truth merciful because Thou art supremely just. Help me, O just and merciful God, for I seek Thy light. Help me, that I may understand what I say! Verily then Thou art merciful because Thou art just. Is then Thy mercy born of Thy justice? Dost Thou then out of justice spare the wicked? If it be so, O Lord, if it be so, teach me how it is so. Is it because it is just that Thou shouldest so be good that Thou could not be conceived better, and shouldest work so mightily that Thou could not be conceived mightier? For what is juster than this? Yet this would not be, if Thou wert good in punishing only, not in sparing; and if Thou madest them good only that were merely not good, and not also those that were evil. And so it is just that Thou should spare the wicked, and make them that were wicked to be good. Lastly, what is not done justly, ought not to be done; and what ought not to be done, is done unjustly. If then Thou dost not have mercy on the wicked justly, then Thou hast mercy on them unjustly: and since it were blasphemy to say this, it is fit to believe that Thou hast mercy on the wicked justly.

CHAPTER X

BUT it is also just that Thou shouldest punish the wicked; for what is more just than that the good should receive good things and the evil evil things? How then is it just for Thee both to punish the wicked and also to spare them? For when Thou dost punish the wicked, it is just, because it is agreeable to their deserts; but when Thou sparest them, it is just also, because though it befitted not their deserts, yet it befitted Thy goodness. For in sparing the wicked Thou are just in respect of Thyself, though not in respect of us; just as Thou art pitiful in respect of us and not in respect of Thyself; since in saving us, whom Thou mightest justly destroy, Thou art pitiful; not that Thou art Thyself moved by the feeling of pity, but that we feel the effect of pity; and in the same manner Thou art just, not that Thou hast rendered to us what we have deserved, but that Thou dost what becomes Thee, the supremely Good. Thus dost Thou without contradiction punish justly and justly spare.

CHAPTER XI

BUT is it not also just even in respect of Thyself, O Lord, to punish the wicked? For it is just that Thou shouldest be so just as no man could conceive Thee juster; and this Thou wouldest by no means be, if Thou didst only render good to the good and not evil to the evil. Far juster is he that rewards the good and evil alike according to their deservings and not the good only. And so Thou art just in respect of Thyself, O just and gracious God, both when Thou punishes and when Thou sparest. Verily then all the paths of the Lord are mercy and truth and yet the Lord is just or righteous in all His ways: and that without contradiction, since those whom Thou dost will to punish, it is not just should be saved: and whom Thou dost will to spare, it is not just should be condemned. For that alone is just, which Thou dost will, and that not just, which Thou wiliest not. Thus then is Thy mercy born of Thy justice, because it is just that Thou shouldest be so good as to be good even in sparing; and this is perchance why the supremely just can will good to the evil. But if it can at all be apprehended why Thou canst will to save the wicked; certainly that can by no means be comprehended why among those alike wicked Thou savest these rather than those by Thy supreme goodness and condemns those rather than these by Thy supreme justice. Thus then hast Thou indeed perception and omnipotence, art pitiful and yet without passion; as Thou hast life, wisdom, goodness, blessedness, eternity and whatsoever other attributes it is better to have than not to have.

CHAPTER XII

BUT certainly whatsoever Thou art, this Thou art by reason of nothing else outside of Thyself. Thou therefore art the life whereby Thou lives; and that wisdom whereby Thou art wise; and that very goodness, whereby Thou art good both to the good and also to the evil; and so with the rest of Thine attributes.

CHAPTER XIII

BUT everything which is anyhow comprehended in place or time, is less than that which no law of place or time restrained. Since then there is nothing greater than Thou, no place or time comprehended Thee, but Thou art everywhere and always: and of Thee alone can it be said Thou alone art uncircumscribed and eternal. How then are other spirits called uncircumscribed and eternal? Thou indeed art alone eternal; because Thou alone of all beings neither beginnest nor ceases to be. But how art Thou alone uncircumscribed? May we say that the created spirit in comparison of Thee is circumscribed, though in comparison of the body, uncircumscribed? For the body is altogether circumscribed, since it is altogether in some certain place, and cannot be at the same time in any other; and this we see only in what is of the nature of body. That again is uncircumscribed, which is altogether in all places at the same time; and this is conceived to be true of Thee only. But that is at once circumscribed and uncircumscribed which being wholly in some certain place, can be at the same time wholly elsewhere; and this we know to be true of created spirits. For if the soul were not wholly in every member of its body, it would not be able wholly to have feeling in every member. Thou then, O Lord, art in a sense wherein it is true of nothing else, at once uncircumscribed and eternal; and yet other spirits also are uncircumscribed and eternal.

CHAPTER XIV

HAST thou then found, O my soul, that which thou was seeking? Thou was seeking God and thou hast found that He is that thing which is supreme among all things, than which nothing better can be conceived, and that this is very life, light, wisdom, goodness, eternal bliss and blissful eternity, and that this is everywhere and always. For if thou hast not found thy God, how can He be this which thou hast found, and which thou hast with so certain an assurance, so assured a certainty understood Him to be? But if thou hast found Him, why dost thou not perceive that which thou hast found? Why doth my soul not perceive Thee, O Lord God, if she hath found Thee? Hath she not found Thee, whom she hath found to be light and truth? Or could she understand anything at all concerning Thee, except by Thy light and truth? If then she hath seen light and truth, she hath seen Thee; if she hath not seen Thee, she hath seen neither light nor truth. Or is it rather that that which she hath seen is indeed both truth and light; and yet she hath not yet seen Thee because she hath seen Thee in part only, but hath not seen Thee as Thou art? O Lord my God, my Creator and Renewer, tell my soul that longed after Thee, what else Thou art beside what she hath seen, that she may see clearly that after which she longed. She stretched out herself that she may see more, and yet seeth nothing beyond what she hath seen, except mere darkness. Nay, she seeth not darkness, for in Thee is no darkness; but she seeth that she can see no farther, because of the darkness which is in herself. Wherefore is this, O Lord, wherefore is this? Are her eyes darkened by her own infirmity, or are they dazzled by Thy splendor? Surely she is both darkened in herself and dazzled by Thee. Thus also she is darkened by reason of her own littleness, and overwhelmed by reason of Thine immeasurable greatness. She is straitened by her own narrowness, and vanquished by Thy vastness. For how great is that Light, whereby every truth shines that doth enlighten the rational intelligence! How vast is that Truth, wherein is contained everything that is true, and outside whereof is only nothingness and falsehood! How immeasurable is that Vision which beholdeth in one glance all things that have been created and whence and by whom and how they were created out of nothing! What purity, what simplicity, what clearness and splendor is there! Surely more than can be comprehended by any creature.

CHAPTER XV

THEREFORE, O Lord, not only art Thou that than which no greater can be conceived, but Thou art something greater than can be conceived. For because there may be conceived to be something greater than can be conceived; if Thou art not that something, there may be conceived something greater than Thee; which is impossible.

CHAPTER XVI

VERILY, O Lord, this is the light unapproachable, wherein Thou dwells; for of a truth there is nothing beside Thyself that can enter into that light, there to behold Thee in Thy fullness. Verily then I see not that light, for it is too great for me; and yet whatsoever I see, I see by means of that light; even as a weak eye seeth what it doth see by means of the sun's light, yet cannot look upon that light as it is in the sun himself. My understanding cannot attain to that light unapproachable; it is too bright for it, it taketh it not in, nor can my soul's eye bear long to be directed toward it. It is dazzled by the brightness, vanquished by the vastness, overwhelmed by the immensity, confounded by the compass thereof.

O supreme and unapproachable Light! O entire and blessed Truth! how far off art Thou from me, who am so near to Thee! How far removed art Thou from my sight, who am wholly present to Thine? Thou art everywhere wholly present, yet I see Thee not. In Thee I move, in Thee I have my being; yet can I not approach unto Thee. Thou art within me and about me, yet I perceive Thee not.

CHAPTER XVII

HITHERTO, O Lord, Thou art hid from my soul in Thine own light and bliss; and therefore she goeth up and down in her darkness and misery. For she looked about her, and beholdeth not Thy beauty. She listened, and heareth not Thy harmony. She smelled and perceived not Thy sweetness. She tasted, and hath no sense of Thy goodness. She touched, and feeleth not Thy smoothness. For Thou hast all these, beauty to the sight, harmony to the ear, sweetness to the smell, goodness to the taste, smoothness to the touch, all in Thee, O Lord God, in Thine own ineffable way, since it is Thou who hast granted to sensible things to have them in their own way which our bodily senses perceive; but the senses of my soul are stiffened and dulled and obstructed by the long sickness of sin.

CHAPTER XVIII

AND once more behold, trouble! So once more cometh sorrow and grief to me that sought after joy and gladness. My soul hoped but now to be filled, and behold, once more is she bowed down by want. I sought to eat and be satisfied, and lo, I am hungrier than before. I strove to rise up into the light of God, and have fallen back into mine own darkness. Nay, not only have I fallen into the darkness, but I perceive myself encompassed about thereby. I fell into it before my mother conceived me. Surely I was conceived in darkness, and was born under the shadow thereof. Surely we all fell in him, in whom we all have sinned. We all lost in him who might easily have kept it and lost it to his own sorrow and ours, that which when we desire to seek, we know not: when we seek, we find not: when we find, is not that which we seek. Help me then, according to Thy goodness! Lord, I have sought Thy face; Thy face, Lord, will I seek; O hide not Thou Thy face from me. Raise me up out of myself unto Thee. Cleanse, heal, quicken, enlighten the eye of my mind that it may look upon Thee. Grant that my soul may collect her strength once more and with all the power of her understanding strive after Thee, O Lord. What art Thou, O Lord, what art Thou? How shall my heart understand what Thou art? Surely Thou art life and wisdom and truth and goodness and blessedness and eternity and everything that is truly good. These indeed are many; but my narrow understanding cannot see so many good things in one apprehension at one and the same time, so as to be delighted by the presence of all at once. How then, O Lord, art Thou all these? Are they parts of Thee, or is rather every one of these wholly what

Thou art? For whatsoever is composed of parts is not in all respects one, but in a certain respect many and diverse from itself; and either actually or in thought can be dissolved: but to be many and not one, or to be capable of dissolution even in thought is far from Thy nature, since Thou art that than which no better can be conceived. Thus there are no parts in Thee, O Lord, nor art Thou many and not one: but Thou art one and the same with Thyself, so that in nothing art Thou unlike Thyself, nay, rather Thou art very Oneness, indivisible by any understanding. Therefore life and wisdom and Thine other attributes are not parts of Thee but are all one, and everyone of them is wholly what Thou art and what the other attributes are. And as Thou hast no parts, so neither is Thine eternity which is Thyself, at any place or time a part of Thee or of Thy whole eternity; but Thou art wholly everywhere and Thine eternity is wholly at all times.

CHAPTER XIX

BUT if Thou was and art and shalt be by reason of Thine eternity; and past being is other than present being, and present being than past or future being: how can Thine eternity be said to be wholly at all times? Or shall we say that nothing has passed away from Thine eternity so as now not to be, though once it was; nor anything to come, as though it were not as yet? Thou then wert not yesterday nor shalt be to-morrow; but yesterday and to-day and to-morrow Thou art. Nay, not even art Thou yesterday and to-day and tomorrow; but Thou art, without any qualification, apart from all time; for yesterday, to-day and to-morrow are distinctions in time; but Thou, although nothing is without Thee, art nevertheless Thyself neither in place nor in time, but all things are in Thee; nothing comprehended Thee but Thou comprehends all things.

CHAPTER XX

THOU therefore dost fill and embrace all things; Thou art before and beyond all things. And indeed Thou art before all things; because before they were made, Thou art. But how art Thou before all things? For in what manner art Thou beyond those things which are to have no end? Is it because they can in no wise be without Thee; but Thou, even though they should return into nothingness, no less art? In this way then Thou art in a manner of speaking beyond them. Or is it again because they can be conceived of as having an end, but Thou canst not? For in this way indeed they have in some sense an end; but Thou in no sense. And certainly that which in no sense hath an end is beyond that which in any sense hath an end. Dost Thou then thus also transcend all things, even though they be eternal, in that Thine eternity and theirs is present to Thee in their entirety, while they have not yet that part of their eternity which is to come, as they have no longer that part which is past. Thus Thou ever transcends them; both in that Thou art always present to them, and because that is ever present to Thee whereunto they have not yet come.

CHAPTER XXI

IS this what we call the age of the age or the ages of the ages? For just as the age of time comprehended all things that are in time, so Thine eternity comprehended the very ages of times themselves. And it is indeed rightly called an age, because it is one and indivisible; but also ages, because of the boundless immensity thereof. And although Thou art so great, O Lord, that all things are full of Thee and are in Thee; yet Thou art such, without being in space, so that in Thee there is neither middle nor half nor any other part.

CHAPTER XXII

THOU therefore alone, O Lord, art what Thou art, and who Thou art. For what is one thing in the whole and another in the parts and has in it anything subject to change, is not in all respects what it is. And whatsoever was not and begins to be, can be conceived not to be; and except something other than itself maintain it in existence, returns into nothingness; and has a past self which is not what now is; and a future self which it as yet is not; that can only be said to exist in a secondary and relative sense. But Thou art what Thou art, because whatsoever Thou art at any time or in any way, that Thou art wholly and always. And Thou art who Thou art in the primary and unqualified sense of the words; because Thou hast neither a past self nor a future self but only present self, nor canst Thou be conceived as at any time not existing. More over Thou art life and light and wisdom and blessedness and eternity and many other such like good things, and yet art but the One Supreme Good, in all respect sufficient to Thyself and needing none beside Thee, while all things beside Thee cannot without Thee have either being or well-being.

CHAPTER XXIII

THIS Good art Thou, O Thou God the Father; this Good is Thy Word, that is, Thy Son. For there can be nothing else in the Word whereby Thou utters Thyself but what Thou art, nor anything greater or less than Thou art; because Thy Word is as true as Thou art truthful. And therefore He is as Thou art, the very Truth; not another Truth than Thyself: and Thou art so utterly without complexity in Thy nature that of Thee there cannot be born anything that is other than what Thou Thyself art. This same Good is the one mutual Love which is between Thee and Thy Son, that is, the Holy Spirit proceeding from both. For the same Love is not unequal to Thee or to Thy Son, because Thou loves Thyself and Him, and He Himself and Thee with a Love as great as Thou art and as He is; nor can that be other than Thou and than He which is not unequal to Thyself and to Him; nor from Thy supreme simplicity of nature can there proceed anything which is other than that from which it proceeded. But that which each Person is, that the whole Trinity, Father, Son and Holy Ghost, is at once; because each by Himself is nothing else than the supremely simple Unity and the supremely one Simplicity, which cannot be multiplied nor can be now one thing and now another. For there is one thing necessary; and doubtless this is that one thing necessary, that wherein is all good, nay rather, which is all good, the one wholly and solely Good.

CHAPTER XXIV

AROUSE thyself, O my soul, and stir up thine understanding and consider so far as thou canst what and how great is this Good. For if particular good things are delightful, consider earnestly how delightful must be that Good which comprehended the pleasantness of all particular goods; and that in a pleasantness not such as we have known by experience in things created, but surpassing that no less than the Creator surpassed the creature. For if the life that is created be good, how good must be the Life that created! If health that is made be pleasant, how pleasant must be that Health that is the cause of all health! If the wisdom be desirable that consisted in the knowledge of things created, how desirable must be the Wisdom that wrought all things of nothing. Lastly, if there be many great delights in things delightful, what manner of delight and how great must these be in Him who made those very things themselves that are so delightful.

CHAPTER XXV

O WHO shall enjoy this Good! And what shall he have, and what shall he lack? Surely whatsoever he wishes he shall have and whatsoever he wishes not, he shall be without. For there shall be goods of body and of soul, such as eye hath not seen, nor ear heard, neither have entered into the heart of man to conceive. Why then, poor child of man, dost thou wander hither and thither, seeking the goods of thy soul and body? Love the one Good wherein are all goods, and it suffices thee. Set thy desires upon that uncompounded Good which is all good, and it is enough. For what dost thou love, O my flesh, what dost thou desire, O my soul? If beauty delight thee, the righteous shall shine forth as the sun: if swiftness or strength or freedom of body which nothing may hinder, they are as the angels of God, because it is sown a natural body, it is raised a spiritual body, spiritual, that is, in powers, not in nature. If a long life of health, there is an eternity of health; for the righteous live for evermore and the health of the righteous cometh of the Lord. If abundance, they shall be satisfied when the glory of God shall appear. If drunkenness, they shall be made drunken with the plenteousness of God's house. If melody, there shall the choirs of angels sing together unto God for ever and ever. If any pleasure, so it be but chaste, Thou shalt give them drink of Thy pleasures as out of the river. If wisdom, the very Wisdom of God shall manifest itself to them. If friendship, they shall love God above themselves and one another as themselves; and God shall love them more than they love themselves; for they shall love Him and one another in Him; and He shall love Himself and them in Himself. If concord, they shall all have one will, for they shall have no will but God's will only. If power, they shall be almighty to do their own wills, even as God to do His; for as God shall be able to do what He willed through His own power, so shall they be able to do what they will through His power; since, as they will nothing else but what He wills, so He shall will whatsoever they will; and whatsoever He willed cannot but be. If honor and riches, God shall set His good and faithful servants over many things; yea, they shall be called sons of God, and gods; and where His Son shall be, there also they shall be, heirs of God and joint-heirs with Christ. If true security, certainly they shall be as sure that those goods, or rather that Good, shall never and in no wise fail them as they shall be sure that they will not lose it of their own free will, and that God their lover will not take it against their wills from them that love Him, and that nothing mightier than God will separate God and them against their wills. But what manner of joy and how great a joy must there be, where there is such and so great a Good! O thou human heart, thou hungry heart, thou heart acquainted with sorrow, nay overwhelmed by sorrow, how wouldest thou rejoice if thou didst abound in all these goods! Look into thine heart and ask it whether it could contain the greatness of the joy which it would have, did it possess so great happiness. Yet surely if another whom thou didst love altogether as well as thyself, were to have the same happiness, thy joy would be doubled, since thou wouldst rejoice for him no less than for thyself. But if two or three or many more should have the same happiness, thou wouldst rejoice as much for each as for thyself, didst thou love each as thyself. Therefore in that perfect mutual love of innumerable blessed angels and men, where none loves another less than himself, each will rejoice no less for every other, than for himself. If then the heart of a man can scarce contain the joy he will have in himself in one enjoyment of so great a good, how shall it be capable of so many and so great joys? And since every man rejoices in the good of any in proportion as he loves Him, as in that perfect felicity everyone will love God beyond all comparison more than he loves himself and all his fellows; so will he rejoice beyond all measure more in the felicity of God than in his own and that of all his fellows. But if they so love God with their whole heart, their whole mind, their whole soul, yet so that the whole heart, the whole mind, the whole soul shall not suffice to the excellency of the love; it will follow that they shall so rejoice with their whole heart, their whole mind, their whole soul, that their whole heart, their whole mind, their whole soul shall not suffice to the fullness of their joy.

CHAPTER XXVI

O MY God and my Lord, my hope and the joy of my heart, tell my soul if this be the joy whereof Thou says unto us by Thy Son, Ask and ye shall receive, that your joy may be full. For I have found a joy that is full and more than full. For when heart and mind and soul and the whole man are full of that joy, yet shall the joy abound yet more beyond measure. Therefore that joy shall not wholly enter into them that rejoice therein; but they that rejoice shall wholly enter into that joy. Tell, O Lord, tell Thy servant inwardly in his heart, if this be the joy whereunto Thy servants shall enter, who shall enter into the joy of their Lord. But assuredly that joy, wherein Thine elect shall rejoice, eye hath not seen, nor ear heard, neither hath it entered into the heart of man. And so I have not yet uttered or conceived, O Lord, the greatness of the joy of Thy blessed ones. For their joy shall be as great as their love and their love as their knowledge. How great shall be their knowledge of Thee, O Lord, and how great their love of Thee! Surely in this life eye hath not seen, nor ear heard, neither hath it entered into the heart of man to conceive the greatness of their knowledge and love of Thee in the life to come. I pray Thee, O God, let me know Thee and love Thee so that I may rejoice in Thee. And if I cannot know Thee, love Thee, rejoice in Thee fully in this life, let me go forward from day to day, until that knowledge, love and joy at last may be full. Let the knowledge of Thee grow in me here, and there be made full; let the love of Thee increase in me here and there be full; so that my joy may here be great in hope and there full in fruition. O Lord, by Thy Son Thou dost command, nay counsel us to seek and dost promise to accept us that our joy may be full! I seek, O Lord, that which by Thy wonderful Counsellor Thou counsellest us to seek; I will accept that which Thou dost promise by Thy Truth, that my joy may be full. O Thou faithful God, I seek; grant that I may receive that my joy may be full. Meanwhile may my mind meditate thereon; may my tongue talk hereof; may my heart love it, my mouth utter it, my soul hunger after it, my flesh thirst after it, my whole substance long for it, until I enter into the joy of my Lord, three persons in one God, blessed for evermore. Amen.

Note on the Argument of the Proslogion.

The argument which Anselm embodied in the Proslogion may thus be stated. Whoever speaks of God, even if only, like the Fool in the Psalms, to say There is no God, must, if he is not content to use words without any meaning at all, attach some sense to the word God. Now the sense in which, as a matter of fact, this word is used, as well by those who deny as by those who affirm the real existence of what is denoted is this: That than which no greater can be conceived. Whoever asserts, however, that this does not exist, involves himself in a plain contradiction. For in asserting that that than which no greater can be conceited does not exist, he implies at once that he can conceive something greater, namely that which, besides being all that this is conceived to be, shall also be real. It would lie outside my present task to discuss this argument at length. But as the reader may fairly ask what is thought of the argument by those who make the criticism of such reasonings their business, I will now add a few observations to what I have already said in the Introduction. I shall not indeed state in detail whether this or that philosopher accepted it or rejected it; for such a catalogue of views and doctrines is by itself a very barren and unprofitable sort of knowledge. But to mention some of the points on which the criticism of Anselm's argument might fasten and has fastened, may well be of use in the way of guidance and suggestion, and this I will do, using technical expressions as little as I can, and assuming as little as I may a previous study of philosophy in my readers.

1. It may be asked, Does the argument , as it stands, prove what it proposes to prove? It is difficult, I think, to deny that it seems to do so, and yet most readers will feel that it leaves them unconvinced. They will be inclined to say of it, as Hume said of Bishop Berkeley's philosophy, that it admits of no answer and produces no conviction. They will suspect some fallacy, some sophistry, they will be sure that it can only be by some trick that they are led so suddenly from the idea or conception of God to belief in His reality, for they are certain that the evidence of reality must be something other than a mere idea. What should it be then? The first answer which suggests itself is probably, The evidence of the senses. Seeing is believing, says the proverb. And in many cases this is true. Who can hold a fire in his hand, asks Bolingbroke in Shakespeare's Richard II., by thinking on the frosty Caucasus? And Kant, the greatest of all the unfavorable critics of the Ontological Argument, suggested that a hundred dollars in my pocket are something very different from any thought of such a sum. But then the most important thing about fire is that it

should warm us; about dollars that they should be handled and pass from hand to hand. This is not so with God. No man hath seen God at any time. He is not an object of the senses at all, but of faith. A vision may sometimes be the means by which faith is won; but it is not the vision in itself that assures us. One may see and yet not believe. They have both seen and hated, said our Lord, both Me and My Father. And again it is written, Blessed are they that have not seen, and yet have believed.

Anselm, for his part, is quite clear that his argument applies to God only. It is not at all his intention to guarantee by his argument the reality of everything of which we may be said to have an idea. His contemporary critic, Gaunilo, thought that the same reasoning would guarantee the existence of a most perfect island; for we can form the idea of such an island really existing; and if the island does not exist, this idea would not be the idea of the most perfect island, since such an island, really existing, would be more perfect still; and we can frame the idea of such an island. But Anselm replied to Gaunilo that his reasoning was only applicable to that than which no greater can be conceived; for such a thing must be conceived to be eternal, without beginning or end; and hence it cannot be possible without being real. It is no part of the notion of an island, even of the most perfect, that it should be without beginning or end. Hence all that our thought of the most perfect island involves is that it is conceivable, possible; that it may exist or have existed or be yet to come into existence; but to speak of an eternal object, one which has no beginning or end, in this way, is absurd. It cannot, if it is not real now, be possible, in the sense that it may have existed in the past or may yet exist in the future; it can only be possible if it actually exists. I see no flaw in this answer of Anselm's to his critic; but it practically admits the insufficiency of the original statement of the argument. For, as originally stated, the argument does but show that our notion of perfection is one which cannot apply to a mere idea, but only to what is real; it does not however prove that there is something real to which it applies. The contradiction lies in thinking of it as unreal and yet as perfect. Nothing is said in the original statement of the idea at first proving only the possibility of its object; and proving the reality of its object only in the case where possibility is inconceivable without reality.

2. We may further ask, however, Does the argument, if not as originally stated proving what it proposes to prove, yet admit of a statement which would prove it? That is, if we give up the notion that the argument, as originally stated, is by itself sufficient to refute atheism, is it sufficient, if we add to it the explanations by which Anselm, replying to Gaunilo, was (as we have seen) led to add to it? I think it is, so long as we do not question the claim of thought to be our only criterion of reality. And few do seriously question this claim. We look into a mirror and see a looking-glass room. Do we believe, like Alice in the fairy-tale, that we should find ourselves in that room, if we could only get through the glass? Certainly not; that, we say, is no real room, it is only a reflection. But why so? We see it as much as we see this room in which we are standing. We see it still, after we have denied that it is real, just as much as we did before. There it is; so is the room on this side of the glass. Where is the difference? We shall find that it is in consequence of the contradictions between them, that we do not think them equally real. On this side of the

glass, if you stretch out your hand to touch what looks solid, it will feel solid, but if you stretch out your hand to something which looks just the same in the looking-glass room, you will feel only the smooth surface of the mirror; if you press on, you will break the glass, and the image will vanish, not by the interposition of anything but by the removal of what seemed to be between us and it. You insist, then, that your world shall be free from contradictions; and so where you find in your everyday experience contradictions between appearances which are alike, you say one is only appearance, a reflection of the other which is real, and so fit both into one harmonious system. It is not otherwise when you rise from the experience of the senses to the higher experience of science. We who believe the Copernican astronomy, and suppose that the earth goes round the sun, not the sun round the earth, see the sun rise in the east and set in the west just as plainly as our ancestors did in the days before Copernicus; but we say that this is only appearance; really the earth is going round the sun, not the sun round the earth. But why really? Because this way of putting it explains more, makes the whole of experience more harmonious than it would be on any other theory.

    And when we are not content even with science; when we indulge ourselves in a faith that, despite the many appearances which are against it, the world is governed by the providence of a good God, we are still in the name of harmony and consistency denying equal reality to appearances which yet remain, as they were before, equally apparent: just as we still see the looking-glass room when we are no longer children, and the sun rise when we have been taught to believe in the Copernican system of astronomy.

The Ontological Argument of Anselm then is, if properly explained, sound, supposing we assume that thought is the criterion of reality; or rather, it is just the assertion that thought is this criterion; that the standard by reference to which we test the reality of everything else is a standard which we carry with us, the standard of what satisfies a thought intolerant of imperfection and contradiction, and insisting, where it finds imperfection and contradiction, that it has before it only appearance and not what can finally approve itself as real; that therefore that is the most real which is the most satisfactory to thought.

3. We may, lastly, enquire whether the demonstration given by Anselm that our thought implies the assurance of this perfect Reality, is precisely what Anselm thought it to be, a proof of the existence of the God of religion? As to this, I will briefly say that it does not seem to me to be so. At least there are few men and perhaps no Christians who will find in what this argument proves to be real all that they need as an object of religious worship. But Anselm did not intend his Proslogionto be taken apart from his Monologion, to which it is a sequel; even if he thought, as he seems to have thought, that the Proslogion would by itself suffice for the refutation of atheism. That I have ventured here to translate the Proslogion without the Monologionis due to the circumstance that the intention of this Selection is not philosophical but devotional; and that the Proslogionis included in it less as a philosophical argument than as an example to show how philosophical reasoning can be made a religious exercise. But Anselm had in the Monologion already determined his conception of the most real as the conception of the best. That than which

no greater can be conceived must be that which our moral consciousness approves as best; for our scale of values is derived from our moral consciousness. Only if an ethical interpretation be given to the conception of the most real will the argument of Anselm lead to the God of religion; but nothing is said of this in the argument itself. For Anselm himself this interpretation was inevitable. His theology was of the school of Plato, and the goodness of God was its fundamental article. But this article itself must be discussed by philosophy; and while it is doubtful, the argument of Anselm will not be found to bring us whither he intended. The understanding at which he aimed, he reckoned to be a half-way house between faith and vision. It presupposed a faith which could count nothing higher in the world or out of it, as Kant says, than the good will: and so it could seem to foreshadow the beatitude pronounced on the pure in heart, that they should see God.

PREFACE TO THE MEDITATIONS AND PRAYERS

THE Meditations and Prayers which here follow, since they are published in order to arouse the reader thereof to the love or fear of God or to self-examination, are not to be read in the midst of turmoil, but in stillness, not quickly but slowly, with close and serious consideration. Nor ought the reader to be careful to read through the whole of any one among them, but so much as he perceives may by God's help do him good in kindling within him the desire of prayer, or so much as may give him pleasure. Nor need he begin any one of them always at the beginning but wherever shall best please him. For to this end are they divided into paragraphs, that anyone may begin or leave off where he chooses; so that the length of a prayer or the frequent repetition of one thing may not become wearisome; but the reader may gather thence some taste of devotion, for to that end were they composed.

MEDITATION I

Concerning the Dignity and the Misery of Human Nature.

I

That we were created in the Image and Likeness of God.

AWAKE, my soul, awake! show thy spirit, arouse thy senses, shake off the sluggishness of that deadly heaviness that is upon thee, begin to take care for thy salvation. Let the idleness of vain imaginations be put to flight, let go of sloth, hold fast to diligence. Be instant in holy meditations, cleave to the good things which are of God: leaving that which is temporal, give heed to that which is eternal. Now in this godly employment of thy mind, to what canst thou turn thy thoughts more wholesomely and profitably than to the sweet contemplations of thy Creator's immeasurable benefits toward thee. Consider therefore the greatness and dignity that He bestowed upon thee at the beginning of thy creation; and judge for thyself with what love and reverence He ought to be worshipped. For when, as He was creating and ordering the whole world of things visible and invisible, He had determined to create the nature of man, He took high counsel concerning the dignity of thy condition, forasmuch as He determined to honor thee more highly than all other creatures that are in the world.

Behold therefore to what greatness thou was created, and again consider what manner of love thou oughtest to render therefore. Let Us make man, saith God, in Our image, after Our likeness. If thou art not aroused by this word of thy Creator, if thou art not at so unspeakable a goodness of condescension in Him towards thee, set all on fire of love towards Him, if thy whole heart is not inflamed with longing after Him, what shall I say? Shall I count thee asleep, or rather dead?

Hearken then diligently what this meaneth, that thou was created in the image and likeness of God. Thou hast here assured to thee sweet matter for devout meditation, wherein to exercise thy thoughts. Note therefore that the likeness of God is one thing, the image another. Thus a horse, an ox, and every other like creature hath some likeness to a man; but none hath the image of a man, except another man. A man eateth, so doth a horse; here is a certain likeness, that is, something in common between natures that are different. But the image of a man none can express, except another man of the same nature as that whose image he is. Thus the image is higher than the likeness.

Thus we may have in the way we have said, some likeness to God if, considering that He is good, we study to be good; if, knowing that He is righteous, we endeavor to be righteous; if, beholding His mercy, we give ourselves to mercy.

But how can we be in His image. Hearken. God is

mindful of Himself, understandeth Himself, loves Himself. And thou too, if thou after thy measure art mindful of God, understands God, loves God, then wilt thou be in His image; for thou wilt be striving to do that which God ever doth. Man ought to make this the end of all his life, to be mindful of the Chief Good, to understand it and to love it; to this should every thought, every motion of the heart be bent, be whetted, be conformed, that with an unwearying love thou should be mindful of God, understand God, love God, and so for thy health set forth the dignity of thy creation, wherein thou was created after the image of God. But why say I that thou was created after the image of God, when, as the Apostle witnessed, thou art thyself the image of God. A man, saith the Apostle, ought not to cover his head, forasmuch as he is the image and glory of God.

II

That the End for which we were created was to glorify God forever. ARE not these inestimable benefits bestowed upon thee by thy Creator enough for thee, to make thee render to Him continual thanksgiving and pay to Him thy debt of love unceasing, when thou considers how at the beginning of thy creation He called thee by His goodness out of nothing, or rather out of the dust of the earth to so great a height of dignity? Apply to thine own life the words of the Saints. Hear what is said concerning a Saint. This then is the praise given to a Saint: With all his heart he praised the Lord. Behold that end whereunto thou was created; behold the task which thy Master hath set thee to do. For to what end should God have raised thee up by so glorious a privilege in thy creation but that

He desired thee to give thyself to His praises without ceasing? Thou was then created to praise thy Creator, so that, being occupied in nothing else than His praises, thou mightest here by the service of thy righteousness draw nearer unto Him and hereafter attain to the life of blessedness. For His praise makes thy righteousness in this world, and thy happiness in the world to come. But if thou praises, praise Him from thy whole heart, praise Him by loving Him. For this is the rule of praising that is given to the Saints: With all his heart he praised the Lord and loved God that made him.

Praise therefore, and praise with thy whole heart, and love Him whom thou praises. For he praises, but not with his whole heart, whom prosperity persuaded to bless God, but adversity restrained from the office of blessing. Again he praises but loves not, who in the praises of God, seeketh to have anything by his praising beside God Himself.

Praise therefore, and praise worthily, so that to the utmost of thy power there be in thee no charge, no thought, no contemplation, no carefulness of mind, that is void of the praise of God. Let no worldly prosperity divert thee, nor any worldly adversity restrain thee from His praise. For thus thou wilt praise the Lord with thy whole heart and with love also; thou wilt seek from Him nothing else than Himself, that He may Himself be the goal of thy desire and the reward of thy labors, thy consolation in this life of shadows and thy possession in the blessed life to come. Hereunto was thou created, that thou should bear a part in His praises for ever and ever, and this thou shalt more fully understand, when thou, being lifted up by the blessed vision of Him, shalt see that by His mere free bounty thou, when thou was not, wert out of nothing created to such happiness, and created, called, justified, glorified unto such unspeakable bliss. For the contemplation of such things will give to thee a love that shall not weary of praising Him forever, of whom and by whom and in whom thou shalt rejoice that thou art blessed with good things so great and so unchangeable.

III

That wheresoever we are, we live and move and have our being in God, so long as e we have Him within us.

BUT leaving that felicity which is to be, with the mind's eye look for a while also upon the greatness of the favor which He hath abundantly bestowed upon Thee even in this transitory life. He who dwelled in heaven, who reigned among the angels, to whom heaven and earth and all that in them is, do reverence, He hath given Himself to be thy dwelling; He hath prepared for thee His presence as an abode, for as the Apostle Paul teaches, in Him we live and move and have our being. Life is sweet, movement is pleasant, being is desirable. For what can be sweeter than to have life in Him, who is the Blessed Life itself? what pleasanter than to order all the course of our will and deed toward Him and in Him who makes us strong with everlasting stability? what more desirable than by prayer and conversation to be continually in Him, in whom alone is true being, nay rather who alone is true being, without whom nothing can have wellbeing. I, saith He, am that I am. This is a saying most excellent. For He Himself alone hath true being, whose being is unchangeable. Thus He, whose being is so excellent, may be said to be in so especial a sense, that He may be said alone in very truth to be; in comparison of whom all being beside His is nothing; when He, I say, created thee for a so great a height of dignity that thou canst not even comprehend the glory of thine own natural dignity, where did He appoint thy dwelling? what abiding place did He prepare for thee? Hear what He saith unto His own in the Gospel: Abide in Me, and I in you. O inestimable dignity, O blessed abiding-place, O glorious intercourse between God and man! How great the condescension of the Creator that it should be His will that His creature should dwell in Him! How incomprehensible the blessedness of the creature, that he should abide in his Creator! How great the glory of the rational creature to have communion with his Creator in so blessed an intercourse, that the Creator Himself should abide in the creature, the creature itself in the Creator! So excellently then were we by His will created, so mercifully was He pleased that we should abide in Him; even He who is above all things, ruling over all things, yet without carefulness; who upholdeth all things, as the foundation of all things, yet without labor: surpassed all things in excellence, yet without pride; comprehended all things in His embrace, yet without distinction of parts; filling all things with His fullness, yet without limitation of Himself.

He then, though He is nowhere absent, chose for Himself a kingdom of delight within us, according to the witness of the Gospel, where it is said, The kingdom of God is within you. But if the kingdom of God is within us, and God dwelled in His kingdom, doth He not abide in us, since His kingdom is within us? Certainly He doth; for if God is wisdom, and the soul of the righteous is the seat of wisdom, then he who is truly righteous has God abiding in him. For the temple of God is holy, saith the Apostle, which temple ye are. Do thou therefore follow earnestly after holiness without fainting, lest thou cease to be the temple of God. He Himself saith of His own, I will dwell in them and walk in them. Doubt not that wheresoever there are holy souls, He is in them. For if thou thyself too art everywhere wholly in thy members, to which thou gives life; how much more is God wholly everywhere, who created both thy self and thy body? Thus it is to be with all diligence considered with what great circumspection and reverence we ought to exercise our senses and the members of our body, over which the Godhead itself presides. Let us therefore, as is right, give to so great a tenant the whole command of our body, so that nothing in us may be displeasing to Him, but that all our thoughts and motions of our will, all our words and works, may wait upon His pleasure, obey His will, and be ordered by His governance. For so we shall be in truth His kingdom, and He will abide in us, and we, abiding in Him, shall live well.

IV

That all we, who have been baptized into Christ, have put on Christ.

AWAKE, I beseech thee, O my soul, and let the fire of a heavenly love be kindled in thy heart, and wisely consider the beauty which Thy Lord God hath bestowed upon thee, and in considering love it, and in loving do it reverence with the service of a holy conversation. For doth not He who makes thee to abide in Him, and hath condescended to dwell in thee, clothe thee, cover thee, adorn thee with Himself? As many of you, saith the Apostle, as have been baptized into Christ, have put on Christ.

What praise, what thanksgiving wilt thou rightly bestow upon Him, who hath clothed thee with so great beauty, exalted thee to so great honor, that thou canst say with all joy of heart, The Lord hath clothed me with the garments of salvation, He hath covered me with the robe of righteousness. It is the highest joy of the angels of God to contemplate Christ, and lo, of His boundless condescension He so far inclined unto thee, as to be pleased to clothe thee with Himself. What manner of clothing is this but that of which the Apostle boasts, saying Christ of God is made unto us wisdom and righteousness and sanctification? How would He more richly apparel thee than by making thee glorious with the garment of wisdom, the ornament of righteousness, the beauty of holiness?

V

That we are the Body of Christ.

AND why should I say that Christ hath clothed thee with Himself, when He hath joined thee so closely to Himself that He hath been pleased to make thee flesh of His flesh in the unity of the Church. Hear what the Apostle saith, expounding the testimony of the Scripture, And they two shall be one flesh. But I speak, saith he, concerning Christ and the Church. Hereupon consider also in how wonderful a bond He hath united thee with Himself. The Apostle established it, that thou art the body of Christ. Ye are, saith he, the body of Christ and members in particular. Keep therefore thy body and thy members with that reverence which is befitting, lest if thou wrong them by lightly entreating them, thou suffer a greater punishment for thine unworthy ill-usage of them, according to the greatness of the reward that would have been thine, if thou has used them aright. Thine eyes are the eyes of Christ. Therefore thou mayest not turn the eyes of Christ to behold vanity, for Christ is the Truth, and all vanity is contrary to the truth. Thy mouth is the mouth of Christ. Thou oughtest not therefore to open, I say not only in slanders and lies but even in idle words, that mouth which should be opened only for the praises of God and the edification of thy neighbor. Be of this mind in respect also of the other members of Christ that are committed to thy charge.

VI

That we are one in Christ, and one Christ with Christ Himself.

CONSIDER also more yet more deeply in how close a union thou art joined with Him. Hear what the Lord Himself prayed to the Father for them that are His: I will, saith He, that as Thou and I are one, so they also may be one in Us. I am (that is) Thy Son by nature; I pray that they may be Thy sons and My brethren by grace. How great a dignity is it for a Christian man, so to grow in Christ that he himself may be called in a sense Christ. This also that faithful steward of God's house hold the Church perceived when he said: All we that are Christians in Christ are one Christ. Nor should we wonder thereat, when we consider that He is the head and we His body;

He the bridegroom and He also the bride; in Himself the bridegroom, but the bride in the holy souls whom He hath bound to Himself in the bonds of an everlasting love. As upon a bridegroom, saith He, hath He set a crown upon Me, and as a bride hath He adorned me with ornaments. Here then, O my soul, here do thou consider His benefits towards thee, be thou inflamed with the love of Him, let the fire that is in thee break out into longing after the blessedness of beholding Him. Cry out boldly in the words of the faithful bride, Let Him kiss me with the kisses of His mouth. Let all delight which is not in Him depart from my mind, let no pleasure, no consolation of this present life comfort me, while His blessed presence is denied to me. Let Him embrace me with the arms of His love, let Him kiss me with the heavenly sweetness of His mouth, let Him speak to me with that ineffable eloquence wherewith He revealed His secrets to the Angels. May the Bridegroom and the Bride enjoy such mutual interchange of discourse, that I may open my whole heart to Him and He reveal to me the secrets of His sweetness. Thus, O my soul, refreshed by these and such like meditations and full of the passion of a holy longing, do thou strive to follow Thy Bridegroom and say unto Him, Draw me after Thee; we will run after the odor of Thine ointments. Speak to Him and speak as a loyal spouse not with the sound of words that passes away but with a longing of heart that fainted not; so speak that thou mayest be heard, so desire to be drawn by Him that thou mayest follow. Say therefore to thy Redeemer and Savior, Draw me after Thee. Let not the sweetness of this world but let thy sweetness of Thy most blessed love draw me. Draw me, for Thou hast drawn me heretofore; hold me fast, for Thou hast laid hold upon me. Thou hast drawn me to

Thee by redeeming me; draw me by saving me. Thou hast drawn me by pitying me; draw me by blessing me. Thou hast laid hold on me by appearing among men, made man for us; hold me fast as Thou sittest on Thy throne in heaven, exalted above the Angels. That is Thy word, that is Thy promise. Thou hast promised, saying: And I, if I be lifted up from the earth, will draw all men unto Me. Draw therefore now in Thy mighty exaltation him whom Thou didst draw to Thee in Thy merciful humiliation. Thou hast gone up on high; let me believe it: Thou reigns over all things; let me acknowledge it. Do I not acknowledge that Thou reigns? Surely I acknowledge it, and give Thee thanks. But do Thou grant that I may acknowledge with the acknowledgment of a perfect love that which I acknowledge by a devout faith concerning Thee. Bind the desires of my heart to Thee with the indissoluble bonds of love, since the first-fruits of my spirit are already with Thee. Vouchsafe that we, whom Thy love in redeeming us did knit to Thee, may have fellowship with Thee in the unity of the same love. For Thou hast loved me, Thou didst give Thyself for me; may therefore my heart and mind be with Thee continually in heaven, and Thy protection with me continually on earth. Help him when he burned with longing after Thy love, to whom Thou didst show love when he despised it. Give to him when he asked, to whom Thou gives Thyself when he knew Thee not. Receive him when he returned to Thee, O Thou who didst call him back to Thee when he fled from Thee. I will love Thee that I may be loved of Thee; nay rather, because I am loved of Thee, I will love Thee more and more that I may be loved the more. May my thoughts be knit to Thee, may my heart be wholly made one with Thee, where our nature, which Thou hast in mercy taken upon Thyself, reigned with Thee in bliss. Grant that I may cleave to Thee without parting, worship Thee without wearying, serve Thee without failing, faithfully seek Thee, happily find Thee, forever possess Thee.

Addressing God in these words, O my soul, do thou kindle thyself, do thou burn, do thou break forth into flames, and strive to become wholly on fire with longing after Him.

VII

A Commemoration of our Sins, for which our Conscience doth reproach us, and whereby we have lost all these things.

BUT when thou considers to what good things and to how great thou hast been by His grace advanced, remember also what good things and how great thou hast lost through thy fault, into how evil a state thou hast by thy sins been cast down. Consider with sighing the evil that thou hast done in thy wickedness; think with groaning upon the good things which thou for that evil's sake hast miserably lost. For what good thing did thy most excellent Creator out of His goodness bestow upon thee; what evil didst thou not render Him, thou that was nurtured in detestable unrighteousness? By losing the good thou hast deserved the evil, nay by casting away the good thou hast chosen the evil; and losing or rather rejecting the grace of thy Maker, thou hast to thy misery increased His anger. Nor canst thou prove thyself guiltless, when the multitude of thy sins, like a mighty army, encompasses thee about; here casting in thy teeth the reproach of thy wicked deeds; there bringing forth a store exceeding great of idle and (which deserve a greater condemnation) harmful words spoken by thee; there again displaying the vast mass of thine evil thoughts. These are those things for whose sake thou hast lost things good beyond all price; for the sake of these hast thou endured to be without the grace of Him that made thee. Groan as thou thinks upon them, renounce them as thou groans, condemn them as thou renounces them, renounce them by changing thy life for a better. Strive inwardly with thyself, lest anon, even for a moment, thou assent to some vanity, whether in heart or in tongue or, what hath the greatest condemnation, even in deed. Let there be in thy mind a daily, nay, a continual warfare, lest thou keep any league with thy sins. Strictly examine thyself always, search out the secrets of thy heart, and whatsoever thou finds in thy self that is reprobate, smite it with severe reproofs, throw it down, crush it, root it out, cast it forth, destroy it altogether. Spare not thyself, be not gentle with thyself, but in the morning (that is, in the contemplation of the Last Judgment, for the Last Judgment followed like the morning light upon the night of this present life) destroy all the ungodly that are in the land(that is, the offences and sins of a worldly conversation) that thou mayest root out from the city of the Lord(which thou oughtest to build within thyself) all wicked doers(that is, all suggestions of the devil, all delights that God hated, all deadly consenting, all perverse deeds). From all such thou shouldest, as a city of God, be purified, that thy Creator may find and take in possession and continually hold a habitation within thee, wherein He may have pleasure. Be not of those whose obstinacy God Himself seems to lament, saying: There is no man layeth it to heart and saith, What have I done? If they are rejected, because they refused to be ashamed for the evil which they have done, and to reprove themselves, wilt thou not take care, in order that thou mayest come soon into the number of the elect, to call thyself to account, to judge thyself, to correct thyself with severe discipline? Consider then diligently in thy meditations the benefits which thy Creator hath bestowed upon thee, wherewith without any merits of thine He hath exalted thee; and call to mind the innumerable evil thoughts words and deeds, wherewith thine unrighteousness unworthily recompensed His kindness, and conceiving great sorrow in thyself, cry aloud, What have I done? I have vexed God, I have provoked my Creator to wrath, I have recompensed His innumerable benefits with innumerable sins.

What have I done? As thou says this, smite upon thy breast, utter thy voice in groaning, pour forth thy tears. For if thou weeps not now, when wilt thou weep? If the turning away of the face of God from thee because of thy sins stir thee not to sorrow, let at least the greatness of the torments of hell, which these same sins of thine have provoked, break the hardness of thy heart.

Return then, return, thou wanderer from the right way, unto thy heart, draw thy foot back out of hell, that thou mayest be able to escape the evil things which thou hast deserved and win back the good things whereof thou art justly deprived. For if thou have respect to those things which are evil in thee, thou wilt find that thou hast lost all the good things which He had bestowed upon thee. Thou must therefore ever turn thine eyes upon the evils within thee, and especially upon those whereof thy conscience most seriously accuses thee, that He may turn away His eyes from them. For if thou by a worthy purpose of amendment dost turn away thy sins, He turned away from them the eyes of His vengeance; but if thou forgettest them, He remembered them.

VIII

A Commemoration of the Incarnation of our Lord, whereby we have recovered all these things.

THEREFORE, that thou mayest be delivered thence, hear the mercies of thy Redeemer toward thee.

Thou was indeed blinded by the fault of thine original sin and couldest not behold the excellency of thy Creator. Encompassed by the cloud of thy sins thou wentest on still in darkness and, driven by the swift waves of the flood of thine offences, was being swept down into everlasting night.

And, behold, thy Redeemer anointed thy blinded eyes with the salve of His incarnation, so that thou, who couldest not look upon God in His glory in the secret place of His majesty, mightest look upon God appearing in the form of a man, and beholding Him acknowledge Him, and acknowledging Him love Him, and loving Him do thine utmost with all thy might to come unto His glory. He was made flesh that He might call thee back to the things of the spirit. He was made a partaker of thy changeableness that He might make thee a partaker of His unchangeableness. He condescended to thy lowliness that He might exalt thee unto His high loftiness. He was born of a pure virgin that He might heal the corruption of thy sinful nature. He was circumcised that He might teach man to cut off from himself all the superfluity of sinful lusts. He was presented in the temple and received by the holy widow, that He might admonish His faithful servants to be continually in the house of God and to endeavor by the practice of holy living to be worthy to receive Him. He was taken into His arms and glorified by the aged Simeon, that He might show forth His love towards gravity of life and ripeness in righteousness. He was baptized that He might sanctify the sacrament of our baptism. In the river Jordan as He bowed Himself to receive baptism at the hand of John, He heard the voice of the Father, and received the Holy Ghost coming upon Him in the form of a dove, that He might teach us that we should abide in humility of mind, and therein be honored by the word of the Father in heaven coming unto us, whereof it is said that His communication is with the simple, and glorified by the presence of the Holy Ghost, who rested upon the lowly. For Jordan signified humility; since, being interpreted, Jordan is their descent. And He was baptized by the hand of John, whose name signified the grace of God, that whatsoever we receive of God, we should ascribe it to that grace and not to our own deservings. After fasting forty days He overcame the devil and his temptations, and was glorified by the ministry of angels, thereby teaching us in the whole time of this present life by refusing the delights of things temporal to trample under our feet the world with the prince thereof, and so to be escorted by the protection of angels. By day He abode with the people preaching the kingdom of God, and edifying the multitudes by His wonderful works and by His words. By night he went into a mountain, and gave Himself to prayer, teaching us, as the season required, sometimes by word and deed to show forth, according to our ability, to our neighbors among whom we live, the way of life; sometimes, entering into the stillness of our soul and ascending the mountain of virtue, to breathe the sweet air of heavenly contemplation and without fainting to direct our thoughts to things above. He was transfigured in the mount before Peter, James, and John, instructing us thereby that if we study like Peter, whose name is by interpretation acknowledging, humbly to acknowledge our weakness, to supplant our sinful nature (for supplanter is the meaning of James), and in faith to submit ourselves to the grace of God (which is the signification of John), we shall to our happiness ascend the mount of heaven, there to behold the glory of Jesus, He Himself our King being also our guide thither. In Bethany, which is by interpretation the house of obedience, He raised Lazarus from the dead, showing that all, who by the earnest endeavor of a good will die to the world, and rest in the bosom of obedience, shall be raised by Him to life eternal. When He delivered His body and blood to His disciples in the mystical supper He humbly washed their feet, teaching us that the sacred mysteries should be celebrated with deeds of purity and devout humbleness of mind. When He was to be glorified by the splendor of His holy resurrection, He endured the mocking of traitors, the cruelty of insults, the shame of the cross, the bitterness of gall, and at the last death itself, admonishing His servants thereby that they who desire after death to attain unto glory must bear the troubles and labors of this present life and the oppressions of the wicked, not only without murmuring, but with love and desire and cheerful welcome to all that is hard in this world for the sake of the eternal reward.

    Upon these glorious and inestimable benefits, bestowed upon thee by thy Creator, if thou worthily meditate, if thou devoutly embrace them, if thou strive with fervent charity to imitate them, thou shalt not only recover the good things which thy first parents lost, but shalt obtain far greater things for ever through the unspeakable grace of thy Savior. For God Himself through the mystery of the incarnation hath become thy brother; and what ineffable joy shall not this cause to thee, when thou shalt behold thy nature in Him so far exalted above all creation!

IX

That we must pray to be delivered out of the horrible pit, out of the mire and clay.

WHAT then now remains but after the due consideration of all these matters to kindle in the mind the desire to inherit so great goods, and with continual supplications to implore Him who created thee to possess them to bring thee out of the horrible pit, out of the mire and clay, and make thee the possessor of blessedness so great? What is that horrible pit, but the abyss of worldly covetousness? what the mire and clay but the filthiness of carnal pleasure? For in the toils of these two, of covetousness and of pleasure, is it that the race of man is miserably entangled and hindered from attaining to the blessed freedom of heavenly contemplation. For in truth the horrible pit is worldly covetousness, which drags the mind that is subject unto its dominion by desires innumerable, as by chains, into the depth of sin, and suffered it not ever to rest. For the mind of man, when oppressed by the yoke of covetousness, is distracted by the love of things visible and driven hither and hither by divers passions. It is wasted by toil in the getting of money, by carefulness in increasing, by joy in possessing it, by fear of losing it, by grief at the loss of it, and by none of these is suffered to see in how great danger it is. This is the horrible pit, which worldly covetousness ceases not to fill with all these great evils. Out of this pit did blessed David rejoice to be delivered, when he gave thanks and said: He brought me out of the horrible pit, out of the mire and clay.

What is the mire and clay? The enjoyment of unclean pleasure. Cry out boldly then with blessed David, and say to thy Creator, Take me out of the mire, that I sink not. Cleanse thy heart from all the pollution of fleshly delight, shut out unclean thoughts from thy mind, if thou wilt escape the foulness of this mire. But when by repentance and confession, by weeping for thy sin and occupying thy heart with holy meditations, thou hast escaped thence, take heed that thou fall not into it again; but with all thy heart utter thy sighing before God, beseeching His mercy that He may set thy feet upon the rock, that is, that thy mind may establish itself upon the firm ground of righteousness by constantly cleaving unto Christ, of whom it is said that He is made unto us of God wisdom and righteousness and sanctification. Pray moreover that He may order thy goings that they turn not back unto wickedness, but may go on steadily in the heavenly way of His commandments, and so hasten without any turning aside to the blessed country of the Angels.

But when His direction shall have lifted thee up, be careful that thou be not slack in singing the praises of the Creator; rather do thou beseech Him of His mercy to put a new song in thy mouth, that with due devotion thou mayest sing a thanksgiving unto our God. It is meet that thou, my soul, when thou hast been brought into fellowship with God by newness of life shouldest break forth into a new song in His praise, despising things temporal, and longing only after things eternal; being obedient to the law of God not from fear of punishment but from love of righteousness. For this is to sing a new song to God, to mortify the desires of the old man, and to follow the way of the new man, which the Son of God hath shown to the world, from mere desire of the life everlasting. He singeth a thanksgiving, who kept in the remembrance of a pure mind the joys of his heavenly country and, being sustained by the consciousness of a holy life and trusting in the gift of grace from above, strives to attain thereunto.

X

A Meditation on the Miseries of this Life.

IN the midst of these meditations, think earnestly upon all the miseries of this present life, and with a watchful heart consider how carefully thou oughtest to live therein. Remember that thou art of his company, concerning whom the Scripture hath said: A man whose way is hid, and whom God hath hedged in with darkness. For truly thou art hedged in with a deep darkness of ignorance, since thou knows not how God will weigh thy works, and canst not tell what thine end will be. No man knoweth, saith Solomon, whether he is worthy of hatred or of love, but all things are kept uncertain even unto the end.
Imagine to thyself a valley deep and dark and all manner of torments in the bottom thereof. Suppose

moreover a bridge cast across this valley, exceeding long but of no more than a foot's breadth. Let a man be compelled to pass over this bridge, so straight, so high, so perilous; let his eyes be blindfolded that he cannot see his steps; let his hands be bound behind him, so that he cannot guide himself by groping his way with a staff. How great would be the fear and distress of mind in such an one! Dost thou think there would be place in his thoughts for cheerfulness, for merriment, for wantonness? I trow not. All pride would be taken from him, all vainglory put to flight, the darkness of death alone would abide in his mind. Imagine moreover a monstrous multitude of savage birds hovering about the bridge and seeking to drag the traveler, as he crosses it, down into the abyss. Will not his dread be multiplied thereby? And what if each plank be at once withdrawn so soon as he hath passed over it? Will not he be stricken thereby by a yet greater fearfulness?

But now consider the signification of this image and let a godly fear and trembling take hold upon thy mind. By the deep and dark valley is signified hell, which is an abyss immeasurable, and terrible with the shadows of most black darkness. There are assembled together all manner of torments. There all that can soothe is lacking; and everything that can appall and torment and distress, is present. The perilous bridge, from which whosoever makes not his passage over it aright is hurled downward, is this present life; wherein whosoever lives ill, descended to hell. The planks which are withdrawn when the traveler hath passed over them are the days of our life; which pass away never to return, but by growing fewer press us onwards toward our end, and compel us to hasten to our goal. The birds that hover about the bridge and beset them that pass over, are evil spirits, whose whole study is to cast men down that are set on the right way, and to hurl them into the depths of hell. We ourselves are the travelers that pass over, blindfolded by our ignorance and bound by the chain of the difficulty of doing good works, so that we cannot direct our steps freely toward God in holiness of life.

Consider therefore whether thou oughtest not in so great a strait to cry out earnestly to thy Creator, so that, being defended by His protection, thou mayest sing in faith among the hosts of thine enemies: The Lord is my light and my salvation; whom then shall I fear? He is thy light against thy blindness; thy salvation against thy difficulty. These are the two evils, where into our first father caused us to fall, even ignorance whither we go and difficulty in seeing what we ought to do. Meditate upon these things, O my soul, think upon them; let thy mind daily exercise itself therein. Let it being intent thereon, turn away from vain and unprofitable cares and thoughts, let it burn with the fire of holy fear and blessed love to fly from these evils and lay hold upon eternal goods.

XI

Of the Body, after the Departure of the Soul.

TO Thee I now turn back, O my most sweet Creator, my most gracious Redeemer, Thou fashioner and refashioner of my nature, humbly in prayer beseeching Thy goodness to teach my heart to consider with life-giving fear and wholesome trembling the foul and mournful state of my flesh after my death when bereft of that spirit which doth at present quicken it, it must be delivered over to be consumed by corruption and the worm. If it have any beauty now, wherein it taketh pride, where will it then be? where the abundance of most exquisite delights? where the delicate limbs? Will there not then be fulfilled indeed that saying of the Prophet, All flesh is grass, and all the goodliness thereof is as the flower of the field? Then shall mine eyes be closed and turned backward unto the inner chambers of the brain, in the vain and mischievous imaginations whereof I so often took pleasure. Now they rejoice to drink in vanity as daylight; but then shall they lie covered with horrible darkness. The ears that now with damnable delight entertain the discourse of slanderers and the vain rumors of the world shall then lie open to the worms, soon to be filled by them. The teeth that now are loosened in gluttonous eating shall be miserably clogged and choked. The nostrils shall stink, that now are delighted with variety of sweet odors. The lips shall be hideous with the fullness of corruption, that so many times rejoiced to be opened in foolish laughter. The throat shall be clogged and the belly filled with worms, that have again and again been swollen by all manner of meats.

But why should I speak severally of every member? The whole frame of the body, whose health comfort and pleasure is almost all our care, shall be dissolved into corruption, into worms, at the last into the basest dust of the earth. Where is now thy proud neck, where thy boastful words, thy rich apparel, thy manifold delights? They have passed away like a dream, they have all gone never to return, and him that was in love with them they have left to misery.

XII

Of the Soul after her Separation from the Body.

O GOOD God, what is it that I behold? Lo, there cometh fear upon fear, sorrow upon sorrow. After she is separated from the body, the soul shall be beset by a multitude of evil spirits, who shall hasten to meet her and shall magnify their accusations against her. And inquisition shall be made concerning all things whereof they accuse her, even to the least of the negligences that she hath committed. There shall come the prince of this world with his companions, raging with fury, cunning in deceit, skillful in lying, malignant in accusing, bringing forth against the soul all that he can of the evils that she hath done, and devising falsely many beside that she hath not done. O terrible hour, O severe judgment! On the one hand will be a Judge most strict in judgment; on the other adversaries most wanton in accusing. The soul shall stand alone with none to comfort her, except she be defended by the consciousness of good works. But in that great severity of judgment, wherein all things shall be laid open, who shall boast that his heart is clean? If the righteous scarcely be saved, where shall the ungodly and the sinner appear? Then shall idle gladness depart, the pomp of place shall be put to flight, the pursuit of worldly greatness shall be proved deceitful.

Blessed is the soul, which in that judgment a good conscience defended, and the remembrance of a holy life protected; which, while she was yet in the flesh, was often cleansed by the water of repentance, adorned with earnestness of confession, enlightened by meditation on

God's holy law; which humility made gentle, and patience quiet, and obedience free from seeking her own will, and charity fervent in the performance of every virtue. Such a soul shall not fear that dreadful hour, and shall not be ashamed when she speaketh with her enemies in the gate. For she will have fellowship with them, of whom the Scripture saith: When He hath given His beloved sleep, behold the inheritance of the Lord.

XIII

A Meditation on the Day of Judgment, wherein the Goats shall be set on the Left Hand.

BUT who can say anything of that terrible sentence of the Last Judgment, whereby the sheep shall be set on the right hand and the goats on the left? How great shall be the trembling when the powers of the heavens shall be shaken? How great the confusion, the lamentation, the crying of those that howl, when they that neglect to do good shall be met by that terrible word, Depart from Me, ye cursed, into everlasting fire. Verily that day is a day of wrath, a day of trouble and distress, a day of wasteness and desolation, a day of darkness and gloominess, a day of clouds and thick darkness, a day of the trumpet and alarm. Verily bitter is the voice of the day of the Lord; the mighty man shall be afflicted therein. For they that in the pride of their hearts despise the will of God, boast themselves now in the following of their own wills; but then shall they be cast into everlasting fire which shall not be quenched forever, and the worm that dieth not shall feed upon them, and the smoke of their torment shall ascend up for ever and ever.

XIV

A Meditation on the Joy which shall be where the Sheep shall be set on the Right Hand.

BUT while these are in woe, and for distress of spirit are uttering the lamentable groaning of their hearts, what thinks thou will be the joy and exultation of those blessed ones, who shall be set at the right hand of God and hear that most blissful voice which shall say unto them, Come, ye blessed of My Father, inherit the kingdom prepared for you from the foundation of the world. Then verily shall the voice of joy and health abide in the dwellings of the righteous. Then shall the Lord lift up the head of the meek, who now refuse not to be counted vile and outcast for His sake. He shall heal the broken hearted, and console with everlasting joy them that weep for longing after Him in this earthly pilgrimage. Then shall be manifested their unspeakable reward, who for love of their Creator rejoice in the renunciation of their own wills. In that day shall a heavenly crown be set upon the heads of them that serve Him, and the glory of those that wait patiently for Him shall shine forth with splendor ineffable. There shall love enrich His faithful soldiers with the fellowship of angels, and purity of heart shall bless them that love Him with the blessed vision of their Creator. Then shall that song be sung by all the elect: Blessed are they that dwell in Thy house; they will be always praising Thee. In which song of praise may He vouchsafe to make us partakers who with the Father and the Holy Ghost lives and reigned God, world without end. Amen.

MEDITATION II

Concerning the Terrors of the Day of Judgment. An Incentive to Tears.

I AM afraid of my life because, when I diligently examine it, I perceive that it is altogether sin, or if, where most is barren, there be any fruit found, it is either feigned fruit or imperfect or in some manner corrupt, so that what there is that displeases not God is yet not pleasing unto Him. Therefore, thou sinner, almost all thy life—nay not almost all, but of a truth all thy life—is either in sin and deserves condemnation, or unfruitful and deserves contempt. But why do I divide what is unfruitful from that which deserves condemnation? For if it be unfruitful, it must therefore be condemned. For we know that the saying is true which He spoke who is the Truth: Every tree that bringeth not forth good fruit is hewn down and cast into the fire.

Nay, if I do anything that profited, it is too little to recompense God for the food and drink which I misuse. But who feedeth a flock which is worth less than the cost of the food which it consumed? Yet Thou, O God, art more gracious than men, in that Thou dost feed me and looks for profit from me, Thy vile worm, Thy sinful one that rotted with the corruption of sin. For more tolerable to a man is the stench of a dog's carcass than to God the soul that sinned; yea, far more foully doth this stink in the nostrils of God than that in those of man. Alas, I am no man but the scorn of men, viler than a beast, baser than a dead carcass. My soul is weary of life; I am ashamed to live, I am afraid to die. What is left for thee, poor sinner, but all thy life through to lament thy whole life, so that it may weep for itself, no part not mourning, no part not mourned?

But this is a marvelous thing, and marvelously is my soul to be pitied therein; that her knowledge exceeded her sorrow so that she rested in security as though she knew not her condition. O thou barren soul, what art thou about? Why sleeps thou, thou sinful one? The day of judgment cometh; the great day of the Lord is near, it is near and passes greatly. That day is a day of wrath, a day of trouble and distress, a day of wasteness and desolation, a day of darkness and gloominess, a day of clouds and thick darkness, a day of the trumpet and alarm.

O bitter voice of the day of the Lord! Why slumbers thou, thou lukewarm soul, meet to be spued out of the mouth of the Lord? He who awakes not, who trembles not at these mighty thunderings, is not asleep but dead. Thou unfruitful tree, where is thy fruit? Thou tree worthy of the axe, thou tree worthy to be hewed down and burned, what are thy fruits? Verily they are thorns and bitter sins; would that the thorns would prick thee with repentance so that they might be broken off, and the bitterness of the sins grow bitterer to thee till they perish altogether!

Peradventure thou thinks some sin of thine but a little thing; would that thy severe Judge thought any sin a little thing! But alas, doth not every sin transgress the commandment of God and dishonor Him? What then? Shall the sinner dare to call his sin a little thing? When is it a little thing to dishonor God? O thou dry and useless branch, worthy of everlasting fires, what wilt thou answer in that day, when God shall require an account of the manner wherein thou hast spent the whole time of life that

He hath allotted to thee, even to the least moment that is past in the twinkling of an eye? Then shall be condemned whatsoever is found in thee, in thy work or in thy play, in thy speech or in thy silence, down to the least thought, nay, thy very living, so thy life is not ordered according to God's will. Woe unto thee! How many sins will rush forth upon thee then of a sudden, as from an ambush, whereof now thou takes no note! yea, more sins and more grievous than those of which thou takes note. How many evil things thou dost, which thou thinks not to be evil! how many, which now thou thinks good, will then be revealed unto thee as sins most black! There wilt thou receive the things done in thy body, according to that thou hast done; then, when the time of mercy shall be past; then, when there shall be no room left for repentance, nor any hope of amendment.

Consider now what thou hast done, and what thou oughtest to receive. If thou hast done much good and little evil, rejoice greatly; if much evil and little good, mourn greatly. O thou unprofitable sinner, are not these thoughts enough to move thee to wail mightily? are they not enough to melt thy blood and marrow into tears? Ah marvelous hardness of heart, that hammers so heavy are too light to break! O profound lethargy, which pricks so sharp are too blunt to rouse! O deadly slumber, which thunderings so terrible are too hoarse to disturb! O unprofitable sinner, well may these things suffice to draw forth from thee a river of tears; well may they suffice to make thee weep dry the fountain of thy tears.

But why must I dissemble, why not utter the greatness and the grievousness of the misery that hangeth over me, why hide it from the eyes of my soul? is it that the woes may come upon me unawares? that the intolerable tempest of wrath should suddenly break forth upon me? Nay this were not expedient for a sinner.

But if I speak, whatsoever I can conceive cannot be compared unto the truth thereof. Therefore let thine eyes weep day and night and keep not silence. Make all the woes thou hast endured hitherto heavier; add terror unto terror, wailing unto wailing; for He shall be thy Judge, who hath been set at naught in all my sins of disobedience and transgression, who hath rewarded me good for evil, and I have rewarded Him evil for good; who is now most patient, but in that day will be most severe; now most merciful, but then most just.

Alas, alas! against whom have I sinned? I have dishonored God, I have provoked the Almighty to anger! What have I done, poor sinner? to whom and how wickedly? Woe is me, woe is me! thou anger of the Almighty, break not out upon me! There is nothing in me that can endure Thine anger, O God. Into what straits am I come! On this side are my sins accusing me; and on that the justice of God making me afraid: above is my angry Judge, below the horrible pit of hell laid open, within my conscience on fire, without the world being burned up. The righteous shall scarcely be saved ; as to the sinner thus taken in his sin, whither shall he turn? I am fast bound, where shall I hide myself; and how shall I appear? To hide myself is impossible, to show myself intolerable. I shall desire to hide myself and hate to show myself, but there will be no hiding-place at all, and everywhere shall I be manifest.

What, ah what will then become of me? Who will deliver me out of the hands of God? where shall I look for counsel? where for salvation? Who is He that is called the Angel of the Great Counsel and the Savior that I may call upon His name? It is none other than He, Jesus Himself, the Judge in whose hands I tremble.

Breathe again, poor sinner, breathe again; despair not, hope in Him whom thou fears. Fly to Him, from whom thou didst flee away. Cease not to call upon Him whom thou didst provoke to wrath. O Jesus, Jesus, for Thy name's sake, do unto me according to Thy name! Jesus, Jesus, forget the proud sinner that provoked Thy wrath, and look upon me the unhappy one that called upon Thy sweet name, Thy pleasant name, Thy name that comforted the sinner and opened to him the hope of blessing. For what signified Jesus but Savior. Therefore, O Jesus, for Thine own sake be a Jesus to me. Thou who didst create, suffer me not to perish; Thou who didst redeem me, condemn me not; Thou who didst make me by Thy goodness, suffer not the work of Thy hands to perish by my own wickedness. I pray Thee, most gracious Savior, let not mine iniquity destroy what Thine almighty goodness hath wrought. Acknowledge in Thy goodness what is Thine own in me; and what is not Thine own, wipe off from me. For what profit is there in my blood if I go down into everlasting corruption? For the dead praise Thee not, O Lord, neither all they that go down into hell. If Thou wilt receive me into the broad bosom of Thy mercy, Thy bosom will not be straightened because of me, O Lord. Receive me therefore, O Jesus my beloved, receive me into the number of Thine elect, that with them I may praise Thee, enjoy Thee, and have my glory in Thee among all that love Thy name, who with the Father and the Holy Ghost art glorious forever, world without end. Amen.

MEDITATION III.

To encourage the spirit not to fall into despair, since if we truly repent, we shall without doubt find mercy for all our sins.

WHEN I look back upon the sins which I have done, and consider the pains and torments which I ought to suffer because of them, I have no little fear. And so, full of trouble and full of dread at the thought of my perdition, I go seeking for comfort wheresoever I may find it. But alas, wretch that I am, I find none. For I know well that I have offended not my Creator alone but together with Him all His creation. Therefore my Creator with all His creation doth condemn me, being grievously offended at my sins; and my own conscience, having knowledge of my evil deeds, doth beset me on every side with accusations. And so I find no comfort, nor do I think that I can readily have any. What then shall I do? whither shall I turn myself? For I am left desolate, and the wickedness of my sins compassed me round about. If I desire to return to Him who created me upright, and call upon His unspeakable goodness to have mercy upon me, then am I greatly afraid lest by so great daring I should move Him to anger against me, and lest He should take a more dreadful vengeance upon my misdeeds, whereby I have not feared to outrage His loving kindness. What then? Shall I remain where I am, desperate and without help or counsel? Hitherto hath my Maker suffered me to live; hitherto He ceases not to provide me with all those things which are necessary to the sustenance of this life: and I find it true by experience thereof that my sins have not up to this day so much prevailed against His goodness, that He should put me to confusion, as I have deserved, or should utterly destroy me. Most surely therefore is He gracious toward me, since He bestowed so great goodness upon me, neither hath sought hitherto to avenge Him of mine iniquities.

I have heard, and according to the witness of those that have had experience thereof, it is a true report that I have heard, that He is the Fountain of Mercy, which began to flow from the beginning of the world, and yet flowed unto this day. He was very merciful, they say, and gracious unto our first father Adam, when he committed that sin of eating the forbidden fruit, in that He condemned him not straightway, as he had deserved, to everlasting perdition, but with patience awaited his amendment, and in His mercy helped him that he might be enabled to return into the favor of Him whom he had offended.

Many times therefore He sent His angel unto him, and unto those who were born of him, warning them that they should return unto Him and repent them of their iniquities, for that He would yet with joy receive them, if with all their heart they would repent them of their sins. But they yet, continuing in their sins and despising His admonitions, added sin to sin, and became as it were beside themselves and abominable in their wickedness, since, being made in honor after the likeness of God, they began contrary to nature to live after the manner of brute beasts. He sent moreover patriarchs, He sent prophets, but not even so would they leave their crooked and perverse ways; but some of them who spoke unto them wholesome warnings, they slew; others they vexed with manifold and strange torments. Yet did He chastise them from time to time, as a merciful Father, not that He, being provoked by their evil deeds, might avenge Himself upon them for their scorn of Him, but that they being corrected might return unto His mercy, who by no means willed the destruction of those whom in His goodness He hath created.

But when neither for often admonition nor for often correction would they return unto Him, the Fountain of Pity could no longer restrain Himself, but coming down from the bosom of the Father, and taking upon Him very manhood, taking upon Him the form of sinners, He began to admonish them in gentleness even then to repent of their sins unto salvation and to acknowledge Him to be the Son of God. For there is no sin so grievous but it may be put away by repentance, so that the very devil himself can no longer remember it. Therefore did sinners, seeing the sweet gentleness of their Creator, begin themselves to run zealously unto the Fountain of Mercy, the Fountain of Pity, and to wash away their sins therein. The Fountain of Pity also Himself began to eat and drink with sinners, began to open to them the sacramental blessings of holy confession, for in true confession all stain of guilt is washed away.

After this, as the time drew near at which He was to suffer for the redemption of sinners, the Jews, from whose stock He sprang according to the flesh, being moved by envy, crucified Him, because He was good and merciful. But He nevertheless even in the act of death did not forget His goodness, but prayed to His Father for His murderers, that He might forgive them this sin; for they know not, saith He, what they do. The Lord that willed not the death of a sinner, but rather that he should be converted and live. in His most sweet goodness makes excuse for them. Whose heart is so hard, whose so strong, that this great kindness of our Creator cannot soften? For when His creature, whom He had created after His own image and likeness, so much dishonored Him, yet did He not avenge Himself, but though dishonored and provoked by their many evil deeds, patiently suffered them and gently admonished them to return to Him without delay. Good therefore and gentle is our Lord Jesus Christ; as is said by the prophet, He willed not the death of a sinner, but that he should forsake his evil ways, and so, repenting of his iniquities, return to the favor of His Creator. Again how merciful He is toward the soul that sinned, He declared by another prophet, exhorting it that even after sinning it should return to Him and find mercy; saying, Thou hast played the harlot with many lovers: that is, Thou that in baptism didst promise to be faithful unto Me, hast polluted thy chastity with many lovers; yet repent and return again to Me, and I will receive thee. Therefore let no sinner despair, when she that played the harlot with many lovers is received again; because no sins of ours can dry up, no wickednesses pollute the Fountain of Pity and Mercy, even Jesus Christ, but ever pure and welling forth with the sweetness of His grace He receives all the weak and sinful that return to Him, and washes them clean from all sins whatsoever wherewith they are stained. And that all sinners and unrighteous men may be assured that they do in truth receive the forgiveness of their sins, if they do but take care to lay aside their sins and to repent, He Himself, the Fountain of Pity, for the love which He had toward them, suffered that very flesh which He took for their sakes, as I above set forth, to be nailed to the cross, that they who were dead in sins and could not otherwise return to life, except they were redeemed by the price of His blood, might look upon the price which was paid for their sins and by no means despair.

When therefore I behold this great goodness of my Lord Jesus Christ, and how so many sinners run to the Fountain of Pity, and none are refused, but all are received, must I alone be without hope, and fear that the very Fountain of Pity that cleanses others should not be able to wash away my sins also? .1 know, I know of a truth, and do surely believe that He who cleanses others can cleanse me also, and if He will, for He is most mighty, forgive me all my sins. But between sinner and sinner there is a great difference, that is between him that sinned more and him that sinned less. Whence I, considering how greatly I have sinned, and by how great unrighteousness my unhappy soul is polluted, perceive that I am not only equal unto other sinners but am a sinner more than any sinner, and above all sinners. For many have sinned, and then left sinning; some, though they sinned often, yet did at some time make an end of doing evil; again others, though they have done much evil, have not failed to do much good also, whereby they have merited either to be wholly forgiven the evil which they did, or have obtained that the pains of hell should be made more tolerable unto them. But I, miserable man that I am, a miserable sinner above all miserable sinners, perceiving and knowing the greatness of the destruction down into which my sin and the pleasure of sin was driving me, have yet not taken care to cease at any time from sins and wickedness, but have ever added sin to sin, and so have lightly and of mine own will plunged myself to my sorrow into the perdition prepared for sin, and, did not the immeasurable goodness of the Lord still bear with me, I ought long since to have been swallowed up by hell. I then, who have lived thus, who have committed so much evil, how shall I dare to run with other sinners who have not done so great evil, unto the Fountain of Mercy? For perhaps, so great is the stench of my sin, that He will not cleanse me, as He cleanses other sinners whose stench is less intolerable than mine. Help me therefore, O Lord Jesus Christ, help Thy creature, although overwhelmed by the greatness of his sins, yet looking upon the work of Thy hands, help him that he despair not; for, as we believe, no wickedness is so monstrous that it can prevail against Thee, if only the sinner despair not of Thy mercy.

Suffer me therefore, O Lord Jesus Christ, suffer me to look upon Thine unspeakable goodness, and declare how gracious and good Thou art toward miserable sinners. I have said it before, but it delighted me greatly, so often as fit occasion served, to remember how great is the grace of Thy sweet goodness toward sinners. For the love of men then, and for their redemption, not of those only who sin more or less, but even of those who sin beyond measure, if they do but repent, Thou didst descend from the bosom of the Father and enter into the womb of the Virgin, and take of her true flesh; and by Thy conversation in the world didst call all sinners to repentance and so, dying according to the flesh, didst restore to them the life which for their sins they had justly forfeited.

And so, when I look back on the evil deeds which I have wrought, if Thou wouldst have me judge myself after my deserts, I am assured of my perdition; but when I have respect unto Thy death, which Thou didst suffer for the redemption of sinners, I do not despair of Thy mercy. That robber, who for his sins was crucified with Thee, was ever in sin up to the time of his departure out of this life, yet, because in the very hour of his giving up the ghost he confessed his sin and cried out upon his fault, he found mercy and was that day with Thee in Paradise. Therefore beholding Thee put to death for the redemption of sinners, Thy hands and feet pierced with nails, Thy side opened by the soldier's spear, the stream of blood and water coming out of that side of Thine, ought I to despair? There is but one thing which Thou wilt have, without which no sinner can be saved, to wit, that we repent us of our sins, and, so far as we may, strive to amend our lives. If we do this, we are sure that if but our last day find us so doing (since we have the example of the robber, who even so won salvation in his last hour) we may, trusting in the unspeakable goodness of our Lord Jesus Christ, fear the accusations of our enemy but little or not at all. Having therefore before our eyes the price of our redemption, that is, the death and blood of our Redeemer, which was shed for the remission of our sins; having also the example of the robber, and of many compassed about by many and great sins, whom the Fountain of Pity, Jesus Christ, in His mercy loosed from them, let us not despair, but run to the Fountain of Pity Himself, in sure and certain hope of obtaining the forgiveness of our sins there, where we see and acknowledge so many and so great sinners to have been washed clean, and let us assure ourselves that we in like manner may be washed clean by the same Fountain of Mercy, if we abstain from our sins and wickedness and, so far as we may, strive hereafter to do good. But to abstain from evil and to do good we are not able by our own power without His help. Let us implore therefore His unspeakable mercy, who was pleased to make us when as yet we were not, that He may grant us in this life, before we go hence, to amend our lives and to cleanse them with earnest sorrow, that this life ended we may be enabled to come unto Him by a straight road, none hindering us, to be with Him in everlasting glory with the choirs of angels and all saints, who already enjoy that glory in joy without end.

MEDITATION IV

Concerning the Redemption of Mankind.

O CHRISTIAN soul, soul raised up from a grievous death, soul redeemed and delivered from a miserable slavery by the blood of God, arouse thy mind from sleep, bethink thee of thy resurrection, remember thy redemption and deliverance. Consider where and what is the strength of thy salvation, occupy thyself in meditating thereon, delight thyself in the contemplation thereof; put away thy daintiness, force thyself, give thy mind thereto; taste of the goodness of thy Redeemer, kindle within thyself the love of thy Savior. With thy mind eat of the honeycomb of His words, with thine understanding suck out their sweetness, for they are sweeter than honey; by loving them and rejoicing therein feed thou upon them, for they are savory and wholesome withal. Rejoice in that eating, be glad in that sucking out of the sweetness, make merry in that feeding upon them. Where then and what is the power and might of thy salvation? Surely it is Christ that hath raised thee up. He, the good Samaritan, hath healed thee; He, thy good Friend, with His own life hath redeemed and delivered thee; even Christ, I say, and none else. Therefore it is Christ that is the strength of thy salvation. Where is this strength that is Christ? He hath horns coming out of His hands; and there was the hiding of His power. Horns He hath in His hands, because His hands are fastened to the arms of the Cross. But what power is there in this great weakness? what loftiness in that great lowliness? what that is honorable in that great humiliation? Verily it is therefore a hiding of His power; it is hidden, because it is in weakness; concealed, because in lowliness; secret, because in humiliation. O hidden power! that a Man, hanging upon the Cross should hang up thereon that eternal death which oppressed mankind, that a Man bound to a tree should unbind the world which was made fast to death everlasting! O concealed loftiness! that a Man condemned with robbers should save men who were condemned with devils, that a Man stretched upon the Cross should draw all things unto Himself! O secret might! that one Soul yielded in torment should draw souls innumerable out of hell, that a Man should endure the death of the body, and destroy thereby the death of souls!

Wherefore, O good Lord, O gracious Redeemer, wherefore didst Thou veil so great power in so great lowliness? Was it that Thou mightest thereby deceive the devil, who by deceiving man did cast him out of paradise? But of a surety the Truth deceives none. He who knoweth not, who believeth not the truth, deceives himself; and whoso seeth the truth and hated it or despises it, deceives himself; the truth deceives none. Was it therefore that the devil might deceive himself? But as the Truth deceives none, so neither doth it go about to make any deceive himself, though, when it permitted it, it be said to do it. For Thou didst not take upon Thyself the nature of man, to hide Thyself from those who knew Thee, but to reveal Thyself to those that knew Thee not. Thou didst call Thyself very God and very Man, and didst show Thyself such by Thy works. The thing was secret of its own nature, it was not of said purpose made secret: it was not so done as to be hid, but so as to be accomplished in due course; not to deceive any, but to be done as it ought to be done. And if it be called secret, that signified! no more than that it was not revealed to all. For although the Truth reveal not itself to all, to none doth it deny itself. Therefore, O Lord, Thou didst do thus, neither to deceive any, nor to cause any to deceive himself, but, that Thou mightest do what was to be done as it ought to be done, Thou didst throughout abide in the truth. Let him therefore that deceives himself in Thy truth, complain not of Thee, but of his own unfaithfulness to truth.

Shall we say that the devil had any just claim against God or against men, on account whereof God must first thus deal with him on man's behalf, before He may put forth openly His mighty power, so that by unjustly slaying a just man, he might justly lose the power which he had over the unjust? But surely God owed the devil nothing but the punishment of his sins; neither did man owe him anything except to overcome sin in his turn, so that as man once through committing sin suffered himself to be easily overcome by the devil, so man should overcome the devil in the very straits of death, by keeping even therein his righteousness unimpaired. But even this too man owed not to the devil but to God only. For the sin which he committed was not against the devil, but against God; neither did man belong to the devil, but man and the devil alike belonged to God. And in that the devil afflicted men, this he did not out of zeal for righteousness, but out of zeal for wickedness; not by the command of God, but by His permission only; because it was required by the justice, not of the devil, but of God. There was therefore nothing in the devil, by reason whereof God ought to have hidden or deferred the operation of His mighty power for the salvation of man.

Was there then any necessity that constrained the Most High so to humble Himself, and the Almighty to accomplish a work with so great labor? Nay, all necessity and impossibility is dependent upon His will. For whatsoever He willed, must of necessity be; and what He willed not, it is impossible should be. Therefore of His free will alone, and because His will is ever good, out of mere goodness did He do this. For God wrought thus, not that He might in this manner, and no other accomplish the salvation of men; but it was the nature of man that required it in this manner to make satisfaction to God. God had no need to suffer things so troublesome, but man had need thus to be reconciled to God. God had no need of this humiliation, but man had need of being thus delivered out of the depths of hell. Now the divine nature neither needed humiliation or toil, nor was capable thereof. But human nature must suffer all this, that it might be restored to that state for which it was created; yet neither human nature nor aught that was less than God could be sufficient to this work. For man is not restored to that state for which he was made, if he be not advanced to be like unto the angels, in whom is no sin; and this cannot be, except he have received remission of all sins, which may not be done, unless full satisfaction have been made for them. Now this satisfaction can only be made, if the sinner, or someone on his behalf, offer of his own to God something which is not due to God, but which surpassed whatsoever is not God. For if sin consisted in the dishonoring of God, and if man ought not to dishonor God, even if it were necessary that everything which is not God should perish, then the unchangeable truth and manifest reason of the thing required that whatsoever sinned should render to God, for the honor whereof it hath robbed Him, something greater than that at the cost whereof he was bound not to dishonor Him. But because human nature by itself had nothing so great to offer, and yet without such satisfaction made could not be reconciled, lest the justice of God should leave within His kingdom a sin for which no satisfaction could be made, the goodness of God came to the aid of His justice, and the Son of God took the nature of man upon Him in His own person, so that in that one person there should be a God-man, who should have a sacrifice to offer, exceeding in value not only everything that is not God, but also every debt that sinners ought to pay to God, and so, owing nothing Himself, should give this in payment for others, who had not wherewith to pay that which they owed. For the life of the man who is God is more precious than everything that is not God; and surpassed every debt which sinners owe for the satisfaction of God. For if the putting to death of this Man exceeded all sins which can be conceived, howsoever many and great they be, so they touch not the person of God, it is manifest that the goodness of His life is greater than the evil of all sins which touch not the person of God. That life this Man who had not incurred the debt of death, because He had no sin, offered freely of His own to the honor of the Father, since He suffered it to be taken from Him for righteousness sake, to give an example to all that the righteousness of God should not be abandoned by us even unto that death, which they must at some time incur as a debt due from them; since He who had not incurred that death, and might without abandoning righteousness have escaped it, yet when it was brought upon Him suffered it freely for righteousness sake. Thus in that Man human nature offered to God freely and not as of debt what was its own, that it might redeem itself in the persons of others in whom it had not that which was due as a debt to offer. In all this the divine nature was not abased, but the human was exalted; the divine was not minished but the human in mercy sustained.

Neither did human nature in that Man suffer anything through any necessity, but through free will alone. Neither was it overcome by any violence, but of its own accord, out of goodness unconstrained, it endured to God's honor and the profit of other men those things which the evil will of others brought upon it not through the compulsion of any obligation, but through the appointment of a wisdom that had power to accomplish its purposes. For the Father did not by His commandment compel that Man to die, but that which He knew would be pleasing to the Father and profitable to men, that of His own free will He performed: for the Father could not compel Him to do that which He had no right to exact of Him; neither could this great act of honor but be pleasing to the Father, which His Son freely offered to Him. Thus therefore He rendered unto the Father a free obedience, in willing freely to do that which He knew would be pleasing to the Father. But because the Father bestowed upon Him this good will, though it were free, yet is it rightly said that He received it as the commandment of the Father. In this manner therefore He was obedient to the Father even unto death; and as the Father gave Him commandment, even so He did: and He drank the cup which His Father had given unto Him. This is the perfect and free obedience of human nature, when it freely submitted its own free will to God's will, and hath then of its own accord carried out in deed that good purpose which God hath not exacted but accepted. Thus this Man redeemed all others, in that He reckoned that which He hath freely given to God, as the debt which they owed to God. And by this price man is not only once redeemed from his faults but, so often as he returned to God in worthy penitence, he is received; yet this worthy penitence is not promised to the sinner. As to that which was done on the Cross, by His Cross hath our Christ redeemed us. They therefore who desire to approach unto this grace with a worthy affection are saved; but they who despise it, because they pay not the debt which they owe, are condemned.

Behold, O Christian soul, this is the power of thy salvation, this the cause of thy liberty, this the price of thy redemption. Thou was a captive and in this wise was thou redeemed. Thou was a slave, and thus was thou made free; an exile and thus brought home; lost and thus found; dead and thus raised up. Upon this, O man, let thy heart feed, this let it inwardly digest, sucking out the sweetness and relishing the goodness thereof, at such times as thy mouth receives the flesh and blood of Him, thy Redeemer. Make this thy daily bread and sustenance in this life, and thy provision for the way, for by this and by this alone shalt thou both abide in Christ and Christ in thee, and in the life to come shall He be thy full joy.

But, O Lord, Thou that didst endure death that I might live, how shall I rejoice in my freedom, seeing it cometh but of the chains that bound Thee? how shall I take pleasure in my salvation, since it is wrought but by Thy sufferings? how shall I be glad of my life, which cometh only by Thy death? Shall I be glad of Thy sufferings and of their cruelty that did these things unto Thee? Or if I grieve for Thee, how shall I be glad of that for the sake whereof these things were done, and which would not be, had these things not been? But indeed their wickedness could have done nothing, except by Thy free sufferance, nor didst Thou suffer them except because in Thy goodness Thou didst will it so. And thus I ought to curse their cruelty, to imitate Thy death and sufferings by fellowship therein, by thanksgiving to show my love toward the kindness of Thy purpose concerning me, and so safely to rejoice in the good things which have been bestowed upon me by those means.

Therefore, thou poor silly man, leave their cruelty to the judgment of God, and consider what thou owes to Thy Savior. Remember how it was with thee, and what was done for thee, and consider how worthy is He of thy love who did this for thee. Behold thy need and His goodness, and see what thanks thou shouldest render Him and how much thou owes unto His love. Thou was in darkness, in a slippery place, in the way that goeth down into the pit of hell, whence is no returning; a huge weight as of lead hanging upon thy neck did drag thee downwards, thy back was bowed down by a burden thou was not able to bear, invisible foes drove thee onward with all their might. Thus was thou without all help and knewest it not, because in this state was I conceived and born. O how was it then with thee? Whither were they hurrying thee? think thereon and tremble, consider and be afraid. O good Lord Jesus Christ, when I was thus set in the midst of these dangers and knew it not nor sought for deliverance, Thou didst shine forth upon me like the sun, and show me in what state I stood. Thou didst cast away that leaden weight which dragged me downwards; Thou didst remove the heavy burden which bowed me to the earth; Thou didst drive away them that urged me forward and didst set Thy face against them in my behalf. Thou didst call me by a new name which Thou gives me after Thine own name. I was bowed together, and Thou didst lift me up to look upon Thy face, saying, Trust in Me, I have redeemed thee, I have given My life for thee; if thou cleave to Me, thou shalt escape the evils which were about thee, and shalt not fall into the pit whither thou was hastening; I will lead thee unto My kingdom, and make thee an heir of God and joint heir with Me. Afterwards didst Thou receive me into Thy care, so that nothing should harm my soul against Thy will; and behold, though I have not stuck fast unto Thee, as Thou didst bid me, yet hast Thou not suffered me to fall into hell, but still looks that I should cleave unto Thee and Thou do what Thou didst promise. Indeed, O Lord, thus I was, and these things hast Thou done unto me. I was in darkness, and knew nothing, not even myself; in a slippery place, because I was weak and frail, and ready to fall into sin; on the road downwards into the pit of hell, because in my first parents I had fallen from righteousness into unrighteousness, whereby is made the descent into hell, and from blessedness into temporal misery, whence one must fall into misery eternal. The weight of original sin dragged me downwards, and the insupportable burden of God's judgment bowed down my back, and mine enemies the devils pressed hotly upon me, that, so far as in them lay, they might make me to sin yet more and so bring upon myself a greater condemnation. Thus was I destitute of all help when Thou didst shine forth upon me and show me in what state I stood. For even when I could not yet understand it, Thou didst teach all this to others who stood in my place, and afterwards to myself, before I sought for it. Thou didst cast away the leaden weight that dragged me downwards, and the burden that was heavy upon my back, and the enemies that urged me to destruction, because Thou didst take away the sin wherein I was born and conceived, and the condemnation thereof, and didst forbid the wicked spirits to do any violence to my soul. Thou madest me to be called a Christian after Thy name; as Christ I confess Thee, as a Christian Thou knows me among my redeemed; Thou hast lifted and raised me up to know and to love Thee; Thou hast made me to trust in the salvation of my soul, for the sake whereof Thou gives Thy life, and Thou hast promised me Thy glory if I will follow Thee. And so, though even as yet I do not follow Thee as Thou didst counsel me, but have done many new sins which Thou hast forbidden, yet still Thou waits till I shall follow Thee and Thou give me what Thou hast promised.

Consider, O my soul, consider earnestly, all that is within me, how much my whole being owed unto Him. Truly, O Lord, because Thou madest me, I owe unto Thy love my whole self; because Thou didst redeem me, I owe Thee my whole self; because Thou makes me such great promises, I owe Thee my whole self, nay more, I owe unto Thy love more than myself, insomuch as Thou art greater than I, for whom Thou didst give Thyself, to whom Thou dost promise Thyself. Make me, I beseech Thee, O Lord, to taste by love that which I taste by knowledge; to perceive by affection what I perceive by understanding. I owe more than my whole self to Thee, but I have no more than this, neither can I of myself render even all this to Thee. Draw me, O Lord, into Thy love, even this whole self of mine. All that I am is Thine by creation, make it to be all Thine by love. Behold, O Lord, my heart is before Thee; it strives, but of itself it cannot do what it would; do Thou do that which of itself it cannot do. Bring me into the secret chamber of Thy love. I ask, I seek, I knock. Thou who makes me to ask, make me also to receive; Thou grants me to seek, grant me also to find; Thou teaches me to knock, do Thou open to my knocking. To whom dost Thou give, if Thou denies him that asked? Who is he that findeth, if he that seeketh is disappointed? What dost Thou give to him that prayed not, if to him that prayed Thou denies Thy love? From Thee have I my desire; from Thee may I have also the accomplishment thereof. Cleave thou unto Him, cleave unto Him right earnestly, O my soul! O good Lord, good Lord, cast her not away! She is sick with hunger for Thy love, do Thou cherish her, and let her be satisfied with Thy loving-kindness, enriched by Thy favor, fulfilled by Thy love; yet let Thy love lay hold upon me and possess me wholly, because Thou art with the Father and the Holy Ghost, the one only God, blessed forever world without end. Amen.

PRAYERS OF ST ANSELM

I

A Prayer of Praise and Thanksgiving to God.

I GIVE Thee thanks and praise, O my God, my Mercy, who hast vouchsafed to lead me unto the conception of Thee, and by the washing of holy baptism to number me among Thy children by adoption. I give Thee thanks and praise, for that Thou hast patience with me in Thine unbounded goodness, waiting for amendment of life in me, who have abounded in sins from my childhood even unto this hour. Thee I praise, Thee I glorify, who by the arm of Thy might hast often delivered me out of many distresses calamities and miseries, and hitherto hast spared me eternal pains and bodily torments. I praise Thee and glorify Thee, for that Thou hast vouchsafed to grant unto me soundness of body, a quiet life, the love, affection and charity of Thy servants toward me, for all these things are the gifts of Thy goodness. Holy of holies, who makes all things holy, I bless Thee, I glorify Thee, I worship Thee, I give thanks to Thee. Let all Thy creatures bless Thee, let all Thine angels and saints bless Thee. Let me bless Thee in all the actions of my life. Let all my frame, without and within, glorify and bless Thee. My salvation, my light, my glory, let mine eyes see Thee, which Thou hast created and prepared to look upon the beauty of Thine excellency. My music, my delight, let mine ears bless Thee, which Thou hast created and prepared to hear the voice of Thy cheerful salvation. My sweetness, my refreshment, let my nostrils bless Thee, which Thou hast made to live and take pleasure in the sweet odor of Thine ointments, My praise, my new song,163my rejoicing, let my tongue bless and magnify Thee, which Thou hast created and prepared to tell forth Thy wonderful works. My wisdom, my meditation, my counsel, let my heart adore and bless Thee forever, which Thou hast pre pared and given unto me to discern Thine unspeakable mercies. My life, my happiness, let my soul, sinful though she be, bless Thee, which Thou hast created and prepared to enjoy Thy goodness.

    Father adorable and terrible, worthy of worship and of fear, I bless Thee, whom I have loved, whom I have sought, whom I have ever desired. My God, my lover, I thirst after Thee, I hunger for Thee, I pour out my supplications to Thee, with all the groaning of my heart I crave for Thee. Even as a mother, when her only son is taken from her, sitteth weeping and lamenting continually beside his sepulcher, even so I also, as I can, not as I ought, having in mind Thy passion, Thy buffetings, Thy scourgings, Thy wounds, remembering how Thou was slain for my sake, how Thou was embalmed, how and where Thou was buried, sit with Mary at the sepulcher in my heart, weeping. Where faith hath laid Thee, hope seeketh to find Thee, love to anoint Thee. Most gracious, most excellent, most sweet, who will bring me to find Thee without the sepulcher, to wash Thy wounds with my tears, even the marks of the nails. Ye daughters of Jerusalem, tell my Beloved that I am sick of love. Let Him show Himself to me, let Him make Himself known unto me. Let Him call me by my name; let Him give me rest from my sorrow.

For my sorrow can take no rest while I am an exile from Thy presence, O my God. Come now, O Lord, reveal Thy face to me, show Thy mercy to those that implore it. We know that Thy resurrection is accomplished, manifest to our eyes Thy blessed incorruption. O Thou wonderful one, above all estimation and comparison, I desired Thee, I hoped for Thee, I sought Thee. Lo, Thou Thyself comes, clothed in purple; Thou art red in Thine apparel. Thou hast washed Thy garments in wine and Thy clothes in the blood of grapes. Thou wounded the head out of the house of the wicked, when Thou wentest forth for the salvation of Thy people.

Abide with us, abide with us until the morning. Let us enjoy Thy presence; let us be glad and rejoice in Thy resurrection. The darkness thickens, the evening cometh fast. May our Sun, the Light eternal, Christ our

God show us the light of His countenance!

But what is this? Alas, my Lord, alas, my soul! Thou lifts up Thine hands. Lo, Thou goes upon Thy way. The heavens meet Thee, the skies are bowed under Thee, a cloud is prepared to receive Thee in Thine ascension. Now shall my tears be my meat day and night. I will feed upon my griefs, I will give my soul to drink of my sorrows. My life shall wax old in heaviness, and my years in mourning. Whom have I in heaven but Thee; and there is none upon earth that I desire in comparison of Thee? With my soul will I desire Thee in the night: yea with my spirit within me will I seek Thee early. Yet in the meanwhile wilt Thou come unto us, O Lord, because Thou art gracious, and wilt not tarry, because Thou art good. To Thee be glory, world without end. Amen.

II

A Prayer to the Holy Spirit.

NOW, O Thou Love that art the bond of the Godhead, Thou that art the holy Love which is betwixt the Father Almighty and His most blessed Son, Thou Almighty Spirit, the Comforter, the most merciful consoler of them that mourn, do Thou enter by Thy mighty power into the innermost sanctuary of my heart, and of Thy goodness dwell therein, making glad with the brightness of Thy glorious light the neglected corners thereof, and making fruitful by the visitation of Thine abundant dew the fields that are parched and barren with long continued drought. Pierce with the arrows of Thy love the secret chambers of the inner man. Let the entrance of Thy healthful flames set the sluggish heart alight, and the burning fire of Thy sacred inspiration enlighten it and consume all that is within me, both of mind and body. Give me drink of Thy pleasures as out of the river; so that I may take no pleasure hereafter in the poisonous sweetness of worldly delights. Give sentence with me, God, and defend my cause against the ungodly people. Teach me to do the thing that pleases Thee, for Thou art my God. I believe that in whomsoever Thou dost dwell, Thou makes there a habitation for the Father and for the Son. Blessed is he who shall be counted worthy to entertain Thee; because by Thee the Father and the Son shall make their abode with him.

  Come, O come, most gracious consoler of the soul that sorroweth, Thou refuge in due time of trouble. Come, Thou cleanser from sin, Thou healer of wounds. Come, Thou strength of the weak, Thou lifter up of them that fall. Come, Thou teacher of the lowly and destroyer of the proud. Come, Thou gracious father of the fatherless, Thou gentle defender of the cause of the widows. Come, Thou hope of the poor, and cherisher of the sick. Come, Thou star of the seafarer, Thou haven of the shipwrecked. Come, Thou that art the only glory of them that live, the only salvation of them that die. Come, most holy Spirit, come and have mercy upon me, and fit me to receive Thee: and graciously grant to me that my littleness may be pleasing to Thy greatness, my weakness to Thy strength, according to the multitude of Thy mercies, through Jesus Christ my Savior, who lives and reigned with the Father in the Unity that is of Thee, world without end. Amen.

III

A Prayer to Christ for my friends.

O SWEET and gracious Lord Jesus Christ, who hast shown unto us such charitable love as no man hath greater, nor can any man have so great; Thou who didst not deserve to die, and yet didst lay down Thy life in Thy goodness for Thy servants, and didst pray even for Thy murderers, that Thou mightest make them Thy brethren and sharers in Thy righteousness, and reconcile them to Thy merciful Father and to Thyself; Thou, O Lord, who didst show this great charity to Thine enemies, didst also command Thy friends to show the like. O good Lord, with what affection shall I call to mind Thine inestimable charity? What reward shall I give for Thine unspeakable benefit? For the sweetness of Thy grace exceeded all affection, and the greatness of Thy benefit surpassed all reward. What reward then shall I give unto Him who created me, and created me anew? What reward shall I give unto Him that had mercy upon me and redeemed me? O Lord, Thou art my God, my goods are nothing unto Thee. The whole world is Thine and all that is therein. What reward shall I, who am poor and needy, who am a worm, who am dust and ashes, give unto my God, except to obey His commandment from my heart. And this is Thy commandment. That we love another.

O Thou that art good as man, as God, as Lord, as friend, as whatsoever Thou art, Thy humble, Thy despicable servant desires to obey this Thy commandment. Thou knows, O Lord, that I am in love with that love which Thou commands. I seek that love, I follow after it, for the sake thereof I, thy poor and needy servant knock and cry out at the door of Thy mercy. And in so far forth as I have already received the sweet alms of Thy free bounty, and love all men in Thee and for Thy sake, though not as I ought, nor as I would, I entreat Thee to show mercy to all men. Nevertheless, as there are some the love of whom Thy loving-kindness hast in an especial manner more intimately impressed upon my heart, I do more ardently wish them well and desire more earnestly to pray for them. Very great is Thy servant's longing to pray for them, O good God: yet he is afraid to appear in the company of his loved ones, because he is guilty before Thee. For with what countenance shall I, who am not worthy to ask pardon for myself, presume to entreat Thy favor for others? And I who anxiously seek others to pray for me, with what confidence can I pray for them? What shall I do, Lord God, what shall I do? Thou bides me pray for them, and my love desires to pray for them, yet while my conscience cries out that I should tremble for my own sins, I am afraid to speak for others. Shall I then disobey Thy bidding, because I have done what Thou hast forbidden? Nay rather, since I have presumed to do what Thou hast forbidden, I will embrace that which Thou hast commanded, if perchance obedience may treat my presumption, if perchance charity may cover the multitude of my sins.

  Therefore I pray to Thee, O good and gracious God, for those who love me for Thy sake, and whom I love in Thee; and for those most earnestly, in whose love toward me and in my love toward whom Thou knows to be the most sincerity. And I do this, O my Lord, not as a righteous man, without fear for his own sins, but as one who is afraid out of his poor charity for the sins of others. Do Thou therefore be loving unto them, O Fountain of love, who commands me to love them, and gives me love toward them. And if my prayer be unworthy to profit them, because it is offered unto Thee by a sinner, let it yet prevail on their behalf, because it is made at the instance of Thy commandment. Therefore for Thine own sake, O author and giver of love, for Thine own sake, not for mine, do Thou show love towards them; and make them love Thee with all their heart, with all their mind, with all their soul; so that they may will, speak and do only those things that please Thee and are expedient for themselves. Too lukewarm, O my Lord, too lukewarm is my prayer, because my love is too little fervent. Yet bestow not Thy benefits upon them, O Thou that art rich in mercies, according to the measure of my slothful devotion; but, as Thy goodness exceeded all the love of man, so may Thine answer exceed the affection of my supplication. Do unto them and concerning them, O Lord, that which is expedient for them according to Thy will, that they may so be guided and protected by Thee at all times and in all places as to come at last to a glorious and everlasting security. Who lives and reigns, with the Father and the Holy Ghost, world without end. Amen.

IV

A Prayer to Christ for my Enemies.

LORD Jesus Christ, Lord of all power and goodness, whom I pray to be gracious to my friends. Thou knows what my heart desired for mine enemies. For Thou, O God, who tries the very hearts and reins, Thou knows the secrets of my heart within me. For it is not hidden from Thee. If Thou hast sown in the soul of Thy servant what he may offer to Thee, and if that enemy and

I have sown there likewise what is to be burned with fire, that also is before Thine eyes. Despise not, most gracious God, that which Thou hast sown, but cherish it and give it increase and bring it to perfection and preserve it forever. For as I could begin no good thing without Thee, so can I neither finish it nor keep it in safety except by Thy help. Judge me not, O merciful God, according to that which displeases Thee in me, but take away what Thou hast not planted, and save my soul which Thou hast created. For I cannot amend myself without Thee, because if we be good it is Thou that dost make us and not we ourselves. Neither can my soul endure Thy judgment, if Thou wilt judge her according to her wickedness. Thou therefore, O Lord, who alone art mighty, whatsoever Thou makes me to desire for mine enemies, be that Thy gift unto them, and Thine answer to my prayer. And if I at any time ask for them anything which transgresses the rule of love, whether through ignorance or through infirmity or through wickedness, neither do that to them, nor fulfil my petition therein. Thou who are the true Light, enlighten their blindness. Thou who art supreme Truth, amend their error. Thou art the true Life, quicken their souls. For Thou hast said by Thy beloved Disciple, He that loves not his brother, abides in death. I pray therefore, O Lord, that Thou grant to them so much love of Thee and of their neighbor as Thou commands us to have, lest they should have sin before Thee concerning their brother.

Forbid it, O good Lord, forbid it that I should be to my brethren an occasion of death, that I should be to them a stone of stumbling and rock of offence. For it is enough and more than enough that I should be an offence unto myself; mine own sin is sufficient for me. Thy servant entreated Thee for his fellow-servants that they should not on my account offend so great and good a Master, but be reconciled to Thee, and agree with me according to Thy will for Thy sake. This is the vengeance which my inmost heart desired to ask of Thee upon my fellow-servants, mine enemies and fellow-sinners. This is the punishment which my soul asked upon my fellow-servants and enemies, that they should love Thee and one another, according to Thy will and as is expedient for us, so that we may satisfy our common Master both as concerning ourselves and as concerning one another and serve our common Lord in unity by the teaching of charity to the common good. This vengeance I, Thy sinful servant, pray may be prepared against all those that wish me evil and do me evil. Do Thou prepare this also, most merciful Lord, against Thy sinful servant like wise.

  Come then, O my good Creator and merciful Judge, and by Thy mercy which passes all reckoning, forgive me all my debts as I in Thy presence forgive all my debtors. And if not yet, because hitherto my spirit doth not so forgive perfectly according to Thy measure but willed so to do and accomplished by Thy help what it can, doing violence to itself, this imperfect forgiveness I offer to Thee as it is, that Thou mayest be pleased perfectly to forgive me my sins and according to Thy power, be gracious unto my soul.

  Hearken unto me, hearken unto me, O great and good Lord, with desire for the love of whom my soul is fain to feed herself, but cannot satisfy her hunger for Thee, to call upon whom my mouth findeth no name that suffices my heart. For there is no word that expresses unto me that which by Thy grace my heart conceives concerning Thee. I have prayed, O Lord, as I could, but my will was greater than my power. Hearken unto me, hearken unto me, according to Thy power, who canst do whatsoever Thou dost will. I have prayed as one weak and sinful, hear me, O hear me, as one mighty and merciful; and grant unto my friends and unto mine enemies not only what I have prayed, but what Thou knows to be expedient for each one, and agreeable to Thy will. Grant to all, both living and dead, the help of Thy mercy; and ever hear me not according to the desires of my heart or the requests of my lips, but as Thou knows and wiliest that I ought to will and to ask, O Savior of the world, who with the Father and the Holy Ghost lives and reigns God, world without end. Amen.

INTRODUCTORY NOTE

THOUGH Anselm had a great reputation in his time as a spiritual guide, his correspondence does not afford many examples of spiritual advice which can be well selected for the purpose of the present volume; although not a few letters of warm affection to those who as young men had attached themselves to him as their master in religion witness abundantly to the depth and strength of the friendships thus begun. I have translated here five letters: two to brother monks, one to his only sister, one to a king, and one to a company of devout women who seem to have formed themselves into a little community under the guidance of a certain Robert, perhaps their parish priest, for pursuing a life of regulated piety, though, as it would seem, not under a monastic rule; and who may perhaps remind us of the household of Nicholas Ferrar at Little Gidding in the seventeenth century.

LETTERS OF SPIRITUAL COUNSEL

I

To Ralph.

BROTHER Anselm to his dear brother Ralph. Although you have forbidden me in your letters to address you at the beginning as Dom Ralph, yet my sentiments towards you constrain me to show myself in the rest of my letters your obedient servant. For I am ready to be the obedient servant of Dom Ralphin the same spirit of love in which I love him as the brother, not of my flesh, but of my soul. And so if you bid me not call you what notwithstanding, in virtue of your superiority of character you really are (if I speak my mind candidly) to me, let me at any rate follow my original wish of calling myself what I really am to you. I will then no longer address you as Dom Ralph and sign myself Brother Anselm, but will address you as Brother Ralphand sign myself your obedient Servant, Anselm.

As to your charitable desire that you should be with me wherever I am, that comes to the same thing as my own hearty wish to be with you wherever you are. And as you ask me for advice how this may be, I pray God to help us so that it may be impossible for it to be otherwise. For, if God shall vouchsafe to hear us, may our life together be by His assistance such that so long as life shall last it may be all one act of thanksgiving to Him. But since neither you nor I are our own; for whether we live or die we are the Lord's; if He, who knows better than we what is pleasing to Himself or expedient for us, shall dispose of us otherwise than we wish, let us endure in patience whatever we perceive to be His pleasure concerning us, if we have resolved not to displease Him. For our life is short, and therefore the time is near when we shall rejoice together in an everlasting union with Him and with one another, if by His grace we take care to pass this brief life in submission to His will in all things. Nevertheless, in the meantime, in whatever places we may be, however near to one another or far from one another, may love ever make our spirits one. As to that, however, which you so anxiously entreat me to beg of Archbishop Lanfranc when he comes from England, that you should be with me, I answer that as I wish you that which I understand to be most pleasing to God and most profitable to you, I will, if I find I can, try to bring it about. Meanwhile do cheerfully the business which you are about: for God loves a cheerful giver.

As to your complaint of being hindered by your business from close attention to reading or prayer, let it be a great consolation to you that charity covereth the multitude of sins. For by your being drawn back another is drawn on; by your carrying of the burden another is relieved; by your being heavy laden another is carried on his way. And remember that the servant who returns with his hands empty, runs quicker; but it is the servant who comes home laden that the whole household meets with greater joy.

Nor is he blamed by any because he came more slowly than the other; but because he is tired by useful work, he is bidden sit down and rest. But if you say that your zeal or diligence are not sufficient for the duty laid upon you, I answer that (taking you at your own estimation, not at mine) one weak eye cannot see as well as two, yet it does not refuse to do what it can, since no other part of the body can do it.

But because my letter is already too long, and your other matters will be better discussed by word of mouth than in writing; for written advice you will find in abundance in Holy Scripture; we will for the while commit them in trust to God and pray earnestly concerning them, looking forward both of us to meeting and agreeing to end our correspondence here.

II

To Herlivin, Gondulf, and Maurice, Monks of Bec sojourning in Christ Church, Canterbury.

TO his brethren and dearest friends, Dom Herlwin, Dom Gondulf and Dom Maurice, Brother Anselm, with the hope that going from strength to strength they may attain unto Christ who is the supreme strength of God.

Since you have all one purpose and I have one desire for you all, I join you together and address you all at once in the same letter. If your kindness remembers what manner of men I always wish to see you when you are with me, you know well enough what manner of men I constantly desire to hear you are when you are away from me. For since, as my conscience bears witness, I have from my heart—I do not say, expended—but wished to expend on all of you the love of a brother and on one of you the care of a father, no interval of land or sea has been able to break off this affectionate regard of mine for you. And so, although you have incentives enough to duly progress in the good course on which you have entered; for you have the counsel and advice of our reverend Lord and Father the Archbishop close at hand, you have that constant custom of private meditation which your monastic profession imposes on each one of you, you have the frequent excitement of zeal by mutual religious conversation; yet my unceasing love for you makes me unwilling you should miss my poor exhortations also, though you are absent from me and need them not. And so I admonish and entreat you, my dearest friends, that nothing may distract the mind from watchfulness over self. Let it anxiously consider what gain and progress it makes every day,—lest which God forbid!—it lose and go backward. For in the practice of virtue, as it is harder to attain something new by effort than to lose something old by sloth, so it is more difficult to recover what is lost by negligence than to acquire what one has not yet been observed to possess. Therefore, my beloved friends, always count what is past as nothing, yet without being ashamed to hold that fast to which you have once attained; and though from infirmity you fail to add anything new thereto, yet always strive to do so, without giving in. For that among many called few only are chosen, we are assured by the word of the Truth Himself; but we are all ignorant how few are chosen, for concerning this that same Truth was silent. And so whoever does not yet live as those few live who are chosen, must either amend his life, so as to set himself among the few; or else have a sure and certain fear of reprobation: but if a man think he is already one of the few, he ought not straightway to be confident that he is chosen. For since none of us knows how few the elect may be, no man can know that he is already one of the few elect, although he be already like the few among the many called. And so no one should look behind him, and think how many are not so far advanced as he in the way to the heavenly country; but one should look steadily forward and anxiously ask himself, whether he is walking as well as those of whose election no one doubts. See then, my dearest friends, that nothing cool the fear of God which you have conceived; but grow more and more fervent from day to day, as though the fire in you was fanned by your unwearying zeal, until it be changed for you into the steadfast light of eternal security.

Farewell, my most loving friends; and I beg you, by the brotherly love you owe me, pray with special earnestness that 1, who exhort you to improvement, may not myself finish that miserable course of failure which I began long since, and now have almost done.

III2

To Burgundus and his Wife Richera, on Burgundius' departure as a Pilgrim to Jerusalem.

ANSELM by the grace of God Archbishop of Canterbury to his dear brother and friend Burgundius and his wife Richera, his own sister, health and the blessing of God, and to the best of his power, his own also.

You have sent me word, my dearest Sir and friend Burgundius, that you purpose to go to Jerusalem for God's service and the health of your soul, and that you wish to have my consent to this, and that of your son, my nephew, Anselm.

I am glad to hear of your good intention and advise and entreat you, if you make this journey, neither to carry with you the sins you have committed nor to leave them behind at home, and to make a resolve of living well for the future, as befits a Christian of your degree. Make then a confession by name of all your sins from childhood upwards, so far as you can remember them. See that you have no sin to charge yourself with in respect of your wife, whose goodness you know better than I; but leave her so that she may have the means of counsel and support, whatever God may do with you, and that she be not driven from your house and estate against her will so long as she lives, but may be able to serve God for the safety of your body and soul, and for her own soul and that of your children. Dispose therefore of all your property as you would do if you knew you were just about to die and to give account of all your life to God.

You ask my consent; I pray God you may always and everywhere have God's consent and counsel and aid and protection in all things.

I charge you, my dearest sister, turn your whole heart and mind to God's service and, as God hath taken from you all pleasure in this life, consider that He has done this so that you may have pleasure in none but Him; love Him, desire Him, think upon Him, serve Him at all times and in all places.

God Almighty ever bless you both.

IV

To Alexander, King of Scots.

TO Alexander by the grace of God King of Scots, Anselm servant of the Church of Canterbury wishes health and promises his faithful prayers and sends him the blessing of God and, for what it is worth, his own also. Both I and the whole society of Christ Church,

Canterbury, thank God and rejoice that God has advanced you by right of inheritance to your father's kingdom after your brother's decease, and has adorned you with a character worthy of your royal dignity. As to your brother who by his holy living deserved to make a good end at his departure by God's mercy out of this life, we pray and will pray for him, as you request us, as for one who loved us and whom we loved, that God may grant to his soul eternal joy in His glory among His elect, and everlasting happiness.

I know that your Highness loves and desires my counsel. And so first praying God that He Himself may so guide you by the grace of His Holy Spirit and give you His counsel in all your acts, that He may bring you after this life to His heavenly kingdom, I advise you earnestly to preserve by His help, from whom you received them, that fear of God and those good and pious habits, which you began to have in youth and even in childhood. For kings reign well when they live according to God's will and serve Him in fear; and when they reign over themselves and do not become the servants of their own vices, but master the impetuosity of these by courageous constancy. For there is no inconsistency between constancy in virtue and royal courage in a king. For some kings, like David, at once lived a holy life and also governed the people committed to their charge with vigorous justice and gentle kindness, according as the matter in hand required. Do you show yourself such that the wicked may fear you and the good love you; and, that your life may ever be pleasing to God, let your mind ever remember the punishment of the wicked and reward of the good which shall be after this life. May Almighty God entrust you and all your actions to none other than to His own gracious government.

As to our brethren, whom we have sent into Scotland at the desire of your brother, who has departed, as we trust, from the labors of this life into his rest, we have not thought it necessary to request your kindness for them, because we know well your good will toward them.

V

To Robert and the Devout Women under his Care.

ANSELM Archbishop to his very dear friend and son Robert and to his beloved sisters and daughters, Saegyth, Eadgyth, Theodgyth, Lufrun, Deorgyth, Godgyth, wishes health and God's blessing, and his own for what it is worth.

I rejoice and thank God for the holy resolution and holy course of life which you have agreed to pursue together in the love of God and in holiness of life, as I have been informed by my brother and son William.

In your kind love towards me, you request of me, my very dear daughters, that I should send you a letter of admonition to instruct you and incite you to goodness of life; although you have with you my dear son Robert, into whose heart God hath put it to care for you in the things of God, and who instructs you daily by word and example how you ought to live. Yet since I ought, if I can, to do what you ask me, I will try to write to you a few words such as you desire. My very dear daughters, every action, whether it deserve praise or blame, deserves it according to the intention of the doer. For the will is the root and principle of all actions that are in our own power, and though we cannot do what we will, yet every one of us is judged before God according to his will. Do not therefore consider what you do, but what you will; take more heed what your will is than what your works are. For every action which is right is right because of the righteousness of the will from which it proceeded; from the righteousness of his will is a man called righteous, and from the unrighteousness of his will unrighteous. If then you wish to live a good life, keep watch over your will continually in great and small things alike; both in those things which are in your own control, and in things which are not; lest it swerve in any degree from the right way. But if you wish to know when your will is right, it is certainly right when it is subject to the will of God. And so when you decide to do or think of doing anything of importance say in your hearts, Does God will me to will this or no? If your conscience answers, Yes, God does will me to will this, and my will herein is pleasing to Him; then, whether you can carry out your will or no, cleave to it. But if your conscience witnesses to you that God does not will you to have this will, then turn away your heart from it with all your might; and if you wish to drive it quite away, put it out of your head and forget it so far as you can. But as to the way in which you may rid yourselves of an evil thought or will, consider and observe this advice which I give you. Do not wrangle with wicked thoughts or wicked wishes, but when they beset you, do your utmost to occupy your mind with some useful thought or wish, until the others disappear. For no thought or wish is ever driven away, except by some other thought or wish which is inconsistent with it. Conduct yourselves then thus towards unprofitable thoughts and wishes, so that by attending with all your might to profitable ones, your mind may come to refuse any recollection or notice to the unprofitable. When you wish to pray, or to engage in any other good meditation, if these thoughts which you ought not to entertain are importunate with you, never consent to give up on their account the good design upon which you have entered, lest the devil who suggests them should rejoice in having made you desist from a good work once begun, but overcome them by despising them in the manner I have described. Do not grieve or vex yourselves because they beset you, so long as by despising them in the way I have shown you, you yield no assent to them; otherwise they may take occasion from your vexation with them to come back into your mind and renew their old importunity. For it is habitual with the human mind for whatever either pleases or vexes it to come back into one's head more frequently than that which it feels or thinks should be neglected.

In like manner should a person who is earnest in a holy resolution behave in the case of any unbecoming emotion whether in the body or in the soul, such as the feeling of lust or of anger or of envy or of vainglory. For these are most easily quenched when we treat them with contempt and refuse to indulge in them, or to think about them or to do anything at their suggestion. Do not fear that such emotions or imaginations will be imputed to you as sins, if your will in no degree associates itself with them; for there is no condemnation to them which are in Christ Jesus, who walk not after the flesh. For to walk after the flesh is to agree to the will of the flesh; and the Apostle gives the name of the flesh to every vicious feeling in soul or body, when he says, The flesh lusted against the spirit and the spirit against the flesh. We shall indeed easily extinguish this sort of suggestions, if we crush their first beginnings, according to the advice given above; but it will be difficult to do it, if once we admit them at all into our minds.

I thank you, my friend and dear son Robert, as well as I can, for your loving care which you take for God's sake of these handmaidens of God; and pray you to persevere heartily in this holy and pious purpose. For you may be assured that a great reward awaits you at God's hands for this holy zeal of yours. Almighty God be ever the keeper of your whole life. Amen. May the Almighty and merciful Lord grant you remission of all your sins and make you ever to advance to better things with humility, and never to fall back. Amen.

www.ingramcontent.com/pod-product-compliance
Lightning Source LLC
Chambersburg PA
CBHW052145070526
44585CB00017B/1988